Daniel Leibee

The Bridegroom extra no. 1

A Dispatch from the heavenly Telegraph, giving a full Interpretation of the

Prophecy of Daniel

Daniel Leibee

The Bridegroom extra no. 1
A Dispatch from the heavenly Telegraph, giving a full Interpretation of the Prophecy of Daniel

ISBN/EAN: 9783337168667

Printed in Europe, USA, Canada, Australia, Japan

Cover: Foto ©ninafisch / pixelio.de

More available books at **www.hansebooks.com**

THE
BRIDEGROOM EXTRA No. 1,

A DISPATCH FROM THE

HEAVENLY TELEGRAPH,

GIVING A FULL INTERPRETATION OF THE

PROPHECY OF DANIEL,

PROVING BEYOND A DOUBT THAT

GOD IS ON THE EVE OF COMING TO SET UP THE KINGDOM OF WHICH DANIEL PROPHESIED.

HE INTERPRETATION WILL SHOW THE MANY CONNECTIONS THIS PROPHECY HAS WITH OTHER PORTIONS OF DIVINE WRIT. IT WILL ALSO SHOW THE CONNECTION THAT OUR PRESENT PRESIDENT, ABRAHAM LINCOLN, BEARS WITH THIS PROPHECY. AT THE CLOSE OF THE ILLUSTRATION, I WILL POINT OUT THE MISSION OF ABRAHAM, AS THE REPRESENTATIVE OF ABRAHAM OF OLD, WHO WAS THE FIRST SPIRIT IN THE TRINITY OF GOD'S NATURAL KINGDOM. AT THE CLOSE OF THE CHAPTER, I WILL NOTICE THE TWO THOUSAND THREE HUNDRED DAYS MENTIONED IN DANIEL 8: 14, IN CONNECTION WITH MILLERISM, POINTING OUT THE STARTING POINT FOR THE TWENTY-THREE HUNDRED DAYS, WHICH THEY HAVE BEEN AT A LOSS TO FIND, SHOWING MOST CONCLUSIVELY THAT THE TWENTY-THREE HUNDRED DAYS WERE PLACED THERE TO PUZZLE THE WISDOM OF THE WORLD.

BY DANIEL LEIBEE.

SAN FRANCISCO.

FRANCIS, VALENTINE & CO., COMMERCIAL STEAM PRESSES, CLAY STREET,
1864.

INTRODUCTION.

THE only apology I have to offer for appearing before you in an extra, instead of a "Bridegroom the Second," will be found in the following:

When I wrote the "Bridegroom" I had no doubt but that a sufficient number of them would be sold to enable me to write out and have published the remainder of my work. But in this I have been disappointed, not having sold enough to pay one fourth the cost of publication. I have always known that God's children have been poor in all ages of the world; but, as we are living in the Golden Age, when the streets of the New Jerusalem were to be paved with gold, I thought that some of God's children might have got a little of the precious metal; but in that, as above, I have been disappointed.

This has led me to make another attempt in the form of an extra, hoping that some of them may fall into the hands of God's children who have a little of the god of the age to spare for this purpose, or in other words, that a sufficient number might sell to enable me to prosecute my work to completion. This pamphlet will contain what will be the seventh chapter in my work, and, if ever published, will occupy its proper position in the work. It will therefore be written out with its reference to other chapters. Let this suffice on this head.

Before proceeding to my illustration, and to be the better understood therein, I must notice the interpretation of Divines in general on the Image placed before Nebuchadnezzar. This is the more imperative from the fact that the toes of the Image are, as it were, the gate for the Lord to enter in order to set up his kingdom, inasmuch as his kingdom is to be set up in the days of the kings who rule the four kingdoms that represent the image.

The account of this Image will be found in the 2d chapter of Daniel, commencing with the 31st verse. This was the image of a man, with a head of gold, arms and breast of silver, belly and thighs of brass, legs of iron, and feet of iron and clay. Daniel's illustration was, Nebuchadnezzar the head of gold, and after him another kingdom, but inferior to his kingdom, and still a third kingdom of brass, which should bear rule over all the earth, closing with a fourth kingdom strong as iron, nevertheless it should be divided, and break in pieces and bruise. The toes of the image are a part of this kingdom, which were of iron and clay, and do not cleave together—not solid, like the feet. And in the days of the four kings which shall rule these four kingdoms, shall the God of heaven set up a kingdom, which shall never be destroyed, and the kingdom shall not be left to other people, but it shall break in pieces and consume all these kingdoms, and it shall stand for ever. Such is a short hand account of the image, and the interpretation of Daniel.

All commentators that I have read, have invariably agreed on the subject of the image, agreeing that the four empires mentioned in Daniel, were the four kingdoms which represented the image, viz: the Chaldean Monarchy, or Babylon, the Medo-Persian Empire, the Grecian Empire, and the Roman Empire. These were the empires which they say represented the image. I will show you in a very short space of time that there is not the first word of truth in it.

First.—The four empires did not exist at the same time, and therefore could not represent the image. Nebuchadnezzar saw the image whole in all its parts, save the toes, and these he did not see at all, but Daniel saw them in the interpretation. Now, as Nebuchadnezzar saw the image connected in its three parts, which united the four different kinds of metals, so the four kingdoms that represent the image must all exist on the earth at the same time, and as this was not the case with those four empires, the interpretation of those men fall to the ground, harmless.

Second.—The image being the image of a man, and a man's head controlling the motion of his whole body as well as the feet, implies not only that those four kingdoms must exist at the same time, but that they must be ruled by one man for a term of years, in both law and gospel, and this could never be the case with four kingdoms that did not exist at the same time, another evidence of the erroneous interpretation.

Third.—These men were wrong for another reason, viz: They destroy the image head foremost, from head to foot, whilst Daniel destroys it from foot to head. Their interpretation makes the seed of destruction in the golden head by a rebellion within the head of gold, in the germ of the Medo-Persian Empire. She conquers the golden head, and places the arms and breast in its place. And thus the Greeks do the same. This places the belly and thighs of brass in place of the silver. The same with the legs of iron, and feet of iron and clay. This forces the whole of the image into the golden head, and nothing visible but the legs of iron, and feet of iron and clay. Thus, in place of establishing the image in four kingdoms, they destroy it all but the legs and feet. Now, suppose you would take a man and jam his whole body into his head, so that nothing of him would appear but his legs and feet, what sort of an image would he be? Just so with the interpretation of these men.

Fourth.—I will now prove that it will be utterly impossible to torture those four kingdoms into the image. In Daniel's interpretation we have the following words, 2d chapter, 37th and 38th verses: "Thou, O king, art a king of kings, for the God of Heaven hath given thee a kingdom, power, and strength, and glory. And wheresoever the children of men dwell, the beasts of the field and the fowls of the heavens hath he given into thine hand, and hath made thee ruler over them all. Thou art this head of gold." You will see by this language that God had given Nebuchadnezzar all the then known world, wherever the children of men dwelled. Hence it took all of the old world to constitute the head of gold. Consequently these four empires were not four kingdoms at all, only one kingdom changing rulers four times by conquest, each one of the four Generals had the golden head in possession, each one had the whole of the then known world in his possession. The new world—this continent—had not at that time been known by the children of men; at least this is implied in the language. In my illustration I will prove to you that this changing hands of the golden head four times makes what is in the Scriptures termed "four heads of the dragon," and not four kingdoms, or empires.

I will here close my remarks on this part of the subject, and pay a special compliment on a recent work written by one Dr. Pitts, a Southern clergyman, I believe. This work bears the title of "Armageddon." I had this work in my hand some two years since, and hastily glanced over it, and found the Doctor took the same views in regard to the four empires as other commentators had taken. But he making closer calculation than others, found out by some peculiar foresight that the Government of the United States was the kingdom of God spoken of by Daniel, which will be farther noticed presently.

The Doctor admits the four beasts seen by Daniel in his first vision (7th chapter) were the types of the four kingdoms which was to represent the image, and that the four empires mentioned above represented the beasts, which made Pagan Rome the beast with ten horns. This other Divines also admit. The Doctor next tells his readers they must keep in mind that Rome is the head of the beast; but he forgot to tell them that the beast was the iron legs, and feet of iron and clay, of the image. He then goes on and states that after Pagan Rome fell into ten kingdoms that those kingdoms represented the horns of the beast. Now, what an absurdity this is. Who ever heard of a beast whose horns grew out after he was dead; most certainly no one. When such a beast can be found then it will be time enough to believe the Doctor. He also says the same in regard to the toes. To this I make the same answer as to the horns. Most certainly no one will say that Pagan Rome was alive as such after she had fell into ten kingdoms. Then of course the beast was dead. Again: Who ever heard of a beast having his horns in the feet; for if the Doctor is correct the horns are in the feet of the beast. Again: The Doctor did not tell his readers that the image was the type of a man as the dragon of the Scriptures, called the eighth, but of the seven, as in Rev. 17: 11. Had he had done this he would have placed the horns of the beast at the knee-joint of the dragon, as he says keep in mind that Rome is the head of the beast, and the beast the iron legs and feet of the image, would place the ten horns at the knee of the dragon. I would like to see a man with horns at the knees, or brains, which may be the same.

Again: The Doctor found out by the same rule of calculation that the independence of the United States was to be declared on the Fourth of July, 1776, at precisely 12 o'clock. He makes the calculation from the prophecy of Daniel, and says that a Christian Republic is the kingdom prophesied of by Daniel, as though Daniel did not know the difference between a Republic and a Kingdom. I would very much like if the Doctor would explain how God did set up this Republic in the days of the kings of those four empires. I would like to know how God or anybody else could set up a kingdom or republic in the days of certain kings, when those kings had been dead more than two thousand years. If any one can tell how this can be done he can raise the "Aquila" without help.

Again: I would like for the Doctor to explain and tell how the setting up of this Republic broke in pieces and consumed all those kingdoms Daniel said that the kingdom set up by the God of Heaven would break in pieces and consume all those kingdoms, and it would stand forever. This Republic does not look much like as though it would stand forever. These are inconsistencies which can never be reconciled.

I will here close my remarks on this subject, promising the reader something more consistent than anything above. You must not understand me as finding fault with these interpretations, or in other words, with the men for making the interpretations. They were all right, and in their proper place—all suitable for the ages in which they were made. Moses put a thick veil over the people, which Paul says is over the people unto this day. The Bible being a book of types, we are now in the days referred to by Paul. Hence this veil cannot be pierced but by the spirit which spoke the Bible in man. So these men are not to blame.

THE DISPATCH FROM THE HEAVENLY TELEGRAPH.

Now, in order to make this dispatch plain to you, I must go back to the first Adam, and trace the subject down, in order to point out the connection between the first and second Adam. As stated in the Bridegroom, Eve was taken out of Adam in the Garden of the Lord; after which, the man was driven out of the Garden, but the woman was not. Gen. 3, 24. This implies that both Cain and Abel were conceived in the Garden. As also proved in the Bridegroom, that Adam was natural, and Eve spiritual, of the Spirit of God; and Cain born to represent Adam, and Abel to represent Eve. Cain kills Abel, because Abel's offering had been accepted by the Lord, and his rejected. God then cursed Cain, as stated, which transferred the spirit of the old serpent upon Cain, and turns him black. He then put a mark upon him, which was the kink in the hair, and thus the three stand—God, Christ, and the Devil. Adam, Cain, and Abel could not stand Father, Son, and Ghost, for reasons which I cannot state here. They only stand a type of Father, Son, and Ghost. This shows that the spirit of the woman was dead in Cain, or the ghost dead in the Devil. Jesus, who had been the first, Adam says, the devil was a murderer from the beginning, and as Cain was the first murderer he was the devil referred to. God then traces the generations of Cain up to where they build cities, and work in iron and brass. Then he leaves Cain and commences with Adam and Eve again. Gen. 4, 25, 26. This brings Adam and Eve on this side of Cain and Abel, or Cain and Dead Ghost, which places them as follows: Cain farthest East, Dead Ghost next, Adam next, and Eve farthest West. Keep these things in mind.

We now come down to the call of Abram and Sarai his wife, when he changes the name of both—one to Abraham, the other to Sarah. They now stand at the head of God's natural kingdom—the Jewish nation— the representatives of Adam and Eve at the head of God's natural man. You can see here the reason God had for tracing Cain up to working in iron and brass, and commencing with Adam and Eve. Placing Adam and Eve on this side of Cain and the Dead Ghost, they could be replaced by Abraham and Sarah without interfering with Cain and the Ghost. You will also see that God does not replace Cain and the Ghost on this side of the flood by call. But he promises Abraham an heir, which was born according to promise, and was the first white child ever born. Now mark. Isaac occupies the same place on this side of the flood that Cain occupied on the other side; he stands first on this side of Mother Sarah as did Cain first on this side of Mother Eve. God now stands in Isaac, and Esau and Jacob are born unto him. He calls Jacob his first born son, after his name is changed, as had been those of Abraham and Sarah. Ex. 4, 22. This lets Esau pass off as Live Ghost for the devil, in the place of Abel. Esau was third with Abraham, as had been Abel third with Adam. This brings Jacob into Esau's place as third with Abraham, and completes the Trinity in the natural kingdom, in Abraham, Isaac, and Jacob, as also gives a live ghost on this side of the flood for the devil. You will also see in this that whilst Abraham is the called of God, Esau is the descendant of God in Isaac. Keep these things in mind.

Before going any farther I will explain why Esau becomes live ghost for the devil. Abel being the third man on earth, he stands as ghost in number, but was only typical, as I shall show in the chapter on the Trinity. God calls Abraham; this restores the spirit of the ghost to him; the spirit of the ghost being the spirit of the woman, which was the spirit of God. Hence we find when Abraham dies the word gave up the ghost, is prefixed to the word death, as in Gen. 25, 8. The same is said of Isaac. Gen. 35, 29. And the same of Jacob. Gen. 49, 33. You will see that the word died is not connected with Jacob's departure. Jacob was the third spirit in the Trinity, and was smooth skin, which means he in the place of the woman. Gen. 27, 11. This shows that God was in Jacob, as the word died is not mentioned there. The same is said of Jesus. He gave up the ghost, but he did not die, which shows that he had been Jacob, and as the smooth skin represented the woman, Jesus must be the seed of the woman, set in type by Abel who represented the woman. Hence the spirit of Abel was represented by Jacob the smooth skin as Ghost for God's kingdom, and will be by Jesus as Holy Ghost for God's spiritual kingdom—the seed of the immortal kingdom. Again: Now, in proof of this, let us go back and see what is said of the first Fathers. It is said of Adam that he lived nine hundred and thirty years and died. The same is said in regard to all the Fathers, as in Gen., 5th chapter. Now, why was it not said that they gave up the ghost and died? The ghost is not named in connection with the death of any of them. Answer, because the ghost was dead before they were born, and dead in the devil, too, at that. This being the case, it was essential that a man should be born as live ghost for the devil. This was brought about by God in Isaac, when two were born at a birth—one as live ghost for the devil, the other as live ghost for God. Now, I hope you will be able to understand the matter.

We now pass on up the Tabernacle in the Wilderness. Ex. 26, 33. Here you will see that the Tabernacle was divided into parts, or apartments, by a veil stretched across it in the centre. The outer, or the first part on entering the Tabernacle, was the Holy, and the inner part, behind the veil, the Most Holy; and in the 27th chapter, 9th verse, is the Court placed on the south side of the Tabernacle. This makes the third apartment. The first represents the Land of Eden, the second the Garden of the Lord, and the third the Land of Nod. This Tabernacle was typical of the natural and spiritual kingdoms of God; whilst the Court was a type of the dragon's kingdom, or the devil's kingdom. The most holy place being in the middle, it stands the representative of Eve, between God and the devil. Eve being of the Spirit of God, it stands as God's place. The Mercy Seat being in it implies that it is God's, and the veil being before this place implies the absence of God for a given time. This is the veil that Moses put over the people, alluded to by Paul, and is the veil over them unto this day, and the only veil that is over the people.

Again : Aaron was chosen as the first spirit in the Second Trinity, and he and his sons were consecrated High Priests before God in the holy place in the Tabernacle. He entered once a year within the veil to make restitution for the sins of the people. They made for Aaron and his sons bonnets for glory and for beauty, as in Ex. 28, 43, and 29, 9. Making bonnets for Aaron and his sons implies that the spirit of the woman, which is the Spirit of God, entered the head of God's natural kingdom, and that his sons were to be his successors. The priesthood was to remain with the descendants of Aaron, who was a descendant of Levi, as well as was Moses.

We now pass on to the prophecy of Daniel, where God gives his kingdom to Nebuchadnezzar, and not only his kingdom but all the then known world, and makes him ruler over them all, as shown above. This mark places Nebuchadnezzar in the spirit of the first Adam, who was Lord of all the then known world. The spirit of the woman being in the head of God's kingdom, and then given to Nebuchadnezzar, makes him the golden head of the image, the image standing the representative of Adam with Eve in him, Eve being the golden head in him, as I shall prove to you before I get through. Nebuchadnezzar standing as Adam with the woman in him, goes right to work and makes a golden god, and sets it up on the plains of Dura. Now, if the woman had not been in Nebuchadnezzar, he could not have generated a god, as did Adam a devil after the woman was out of him. You will see now from this forward that it will be all a spiritual matter, represented by kingdoms, and not by the birth of children, natural.

In the 3d chapter will be found an account of the Golden Image ; it was sixty cubits high and six cubits broad. This was a monster of a god to worship ; but, nevertheless, all the then known world was called on to fall down and worship this god, and they all obeyed except the four Hebrews, three of whom were cast into the fiery furnace, heated seven times hotter than was wont to be, out of which they came not having the smell of fire about them. A fourth person was seen in the furnace, like unto the Son of God. This personage was the type of Jesus, and was the protection of the three Hebrews, of the same spirit given to Nebuchadnezzar, which constituted him the Golden Head of the Image. Keep these things in mind.

In the 4th chapter, Nebuchadnezzar has another dream, in which he becomes a Great Tree, whose hight reached up to Heaven, and the sight thereof to the ends of the earth. A watcher, a holy one, came down from Heaven, and cut the tree down, and left an iron and brass band on the stump of the tree, in the tender grass of the field, when Nebuchadnezzar became a beast for seven years, after which his reason returned to him again, when he acknowledged the God of Daniel, saying, that He ruled the armies of Heaven as well as the inhabitants of earth, and none could stay his hand, or say unto Him, What doest Thou ? Now, remark, Nebuchadnezzar is no longer the Golden Head of the Image, but a beast, and consequently a beast's head from this out. I will show you this whole matter to be typical, and that Nebuchadnezzar, from that time, stands in the spirit of Cain, who had the spirit of the serpent transferred to him, and was more subtle than any beast of the field. This places Nebuchadnezzar in the spirit of the devil.

In the 5th chapter, we find Nebuchadnezzar takes his father's throne. This Belshazzar stands in the place of the Dead Ghost in connection with Nebuchadnezzar. Had not a Live Ghost for the devil descended from God in Isaac, in Esau, Nebuchadnezzar could have had no son to take his place. Hence he stands as Live Ghost for Nebuchadnezzar. He did not occupy the throne long before he made a great feast to his lords, when he drank wine with his wives and concubines out of the cups of the Lord's House, when the hand-writing was seen on the wall of his palace. This made the joints of his loins loose, and his knees smote one against the other. Daniel interpreted the hand-writing on the wall, the sum of which was, Belshazzar was "weighed in the balance and found wanting, and his kingdom given to the Medes and Persians," and that night was Belshazzar slain.

In the 6th chapter, we have an account of Daniel himself being cast into the lions' den. He was put in at the mouth of the den, and a stone was rolled to the mouth of the den and sealed with the signet of the king, and the signet of his Lords. Next morning Daniel was taken out unharmed, and his accusers cast in, when their bones were broken ere they came to the ground. Keep all these things in mind, as I shall notice them all in their proper place.

We now come to the 7th chap., in which is the account of Daniel's first vision. In this vision, he saw four beasts rise up out of the sea, diverse one from another. The first was like a lion, and had eagle's wings. The second was like unto a bear, and had three ribs in his mouth. A third beast like unto a leopard, and had four wings like unto a fowl, and had four heads, and dominion was given unto it. The fourth beast was not like any other beast, but it had ten horns, and it had great iron teeth. And among the ten horns sprung up a little horn which plucked up three of the other horns by the roots. As I shall have to refer to all these things again, I run over them hastily. I shall prove to you that these four beasts were the types of the four kingdoms which were to represent the image, and that those four kingdoms are now in existence, in Papal Rome, Spain, France and England. England is the beast with ten horns, and the little horn, and not Pagan Rome.

In the 7th chapter, 10th verse, thrones were cast down, and the Ancient of days did sit. These were the thrones of this Union, as I shall prove. The 11th contains the account of the destruction of the beast, and its being given to the burning flames, for the great words which the little horn spake. 12th. The rest of the beasts had their dominions taken away, and their lives prolonged for a season and time. 13th. Daniel saw in the night-vision, and, behold, one like the Son of Man came in the clouds of heaven, and came to the Ancient of days, and they brought Him near before him. And there was given Him a great dominion, that all people, nations, and languages, should serve him. Here you must keep in mind that Daniel saw this coming in the cloud, in the same night-vision in which he saw the four beasts, in which he also saw the thrones cast down.

17th and 18th verses. These great beasts, which are four, are four kings, which shall arise out of the earth. But the Saints of the Most High shall take the kingdom, and possess the kingdom forever, even for ever and ever. Here you will see that the four beasts were four kings.

Daniel being dissatisfied with this short explanation of his vision, propounded several queries in regard to things that he saw, and was very desirous to know more about the fourth beast, to which the messenger replied thus, saying: "The fourth beast shall be the fourth kingdom upon earth, which shall be diverse from all kingdoms, and shall devour the whole earth, and tread it down and break it in pieces. And the ten horns are ten kings that shall arise, and another shall arise after them, and he shall be diverse from the first, and he shall subdue three kings."

23d and 24th verses. This mark, is the same beast with ten horns, and the little horn. It is here called a kingdom, showing that beasts saw in visions, are a type of kings as well as kingdoms. The messenger then proceeds to the end of the chapter, saying, The little horn shall speak great words against the Most High, and think to change times and laws, and they shall be given into his hand, until a time and times and the dividing of time. But the judgment shall sit and take away his dominion, to consume and destroy it unto the end. And the kingdom and dominion, and the greatness of the kingdom under the whole heaven shall be given unto the saints of the Most High, whose kingdom is an everlasting kingdom, and all dominions shall serve and obey him. Hitherto is the end of the matter. All this will be fully explained before I close.

In the 8th chapter is an account of a second vision. This vision is called the vision of the ram and goat. This vision was in the third year of Belshazzar, whilst the first vision was in the first year of Belshazzar. This ram and goat had a great struggle, but finally the goat proved too powerful for the ram and broke his two horns, completely conquering him. Then the goat waxed very great, and became very strong, but he found his match and his great horn was broken, and for it came up four notable ones toward the four winds of heaven. And out of one of them came forth a little horn, which waxed exceedingly great, toward the south, and toward the east, and toward the pleasant land. Now here keep in mind, that these four horns came up out of the same goat's head, in which the great and notable horn had been broken off, and that a little horn came out of one of these horns. These four horns I shall show you is a second type of the four kingdoms which should constitute the image, and the little horn coming out of one of them the same as the one which sprung up among the ten horns, and the four beasts were a type of these four horns, as will be shown presently.

Daniel then goes on and tells in short hand what great work this little horn done, using almost the same language used by the messenger in the first vision after the queries of Daniel put to the messenger, and closes with the taking away of the sacrifice, and the transgression of desolation, to give both the sanctuary and the host to be trodden under-foot. Then comes in the two thousand three hundred days, overheard by Daniel. Here keep in mind that Daniel saw all this in the vision. The angel or messenger spoken of in the first vision, told him nothing of all in this chapter to the 19th verse. Daniel gives it as what he saw in the vision.

Commencing with the 19th verse, the Angel Gabriel spake unto Daniel, saying, "And he said, behold, I will make thee know what shall be in the last end of the indignation, for at the time appointed the end shall be. The ram which thou sawest having two horns are the kings of Media and Persia. And the rough goat is the king of Grecia, and the great horn that is between his eyes, is the first king. Now that being broken, whereas four stood up for it, four kingdoms shall stand up out of the nation, but not in his power." 19 to 22 inclusive. Here you see the Angel Gabriel makes those four horns four kingdoms, but they shall not stand in their own power. Thus, you see, if these are the kingdoms that are to constitute the image, they are to stand in some other power, and not in their own.

Then the angel continues from the 23d to the 25th verse, inclusive, as follows: "And in the latter time of their kingdom, when the transgressors are come to the full, a king of fierce countenance shall stand up.

This king will understand dark sentences. And his power shall be mighty, but not by his own power, and he shall destroy wonderfully, and shall prosper and practice, and shall destroy the mighty and the holy people. And through his policy, also, he shall cause craft to prosper in his hand, and he shall magnify himself in his heart, and by peace shall destroy many; he shall also stand up against the Prince of princes, but he shall be broken without hand." This is the account of a mighty king that shall stand up in the latter time of these four kingdoms. "This king," the angel says, "shall understand dark sentences, and do great exploits, but not by his own power." This great king, I shall prove to you, to be Old Napoleon. If I succeed in this, you may rest assured that the latter time of those four kingdoms was at hand in his day, and that the transgressor is now "come to the full," and that Louis Napoleon must make the letter to the type set by his uncle, which will cleanse the sanctuary by the close of the year seventy-one, which will be time, times and the dividing of time, from the time of the setting up of the abomination that maketh desolate, as in 8th chapter, 25th verse. Now keep these things in mind, whilst I proceed farther.

We now proceed to the 10th chapter. 1st verse. In the third year of Cyrus, king of Persia, a thing was revealed unto Daniel, whose name was Belteshazzar, and the thing was true, but the time was long, and he understood the thing, and had understanding of the vision. 5th and 6th verses. "Then I lifted up mine eyes and looked, and beheld a certain man clothed in linen, whose loins were girded with fine gold of Zephyr. His body was like the beyrl, and his face the appearance of lightning, and his eyes as lamps of fire, and his arms and feet like, in color, to polished brass, and the voice of his words like the voice of a multitude." You will see here that Daniel had another and third vision, which represents the Trinity. This was also in the third year of king Cyrus' reign, which also represents the Trinity. He describes the personage seen by him, not unlike the Revelator describes the personage seen by him in the midst of the seven golden candlesticks, and no doubt, the persons are the same, spoken in the two men by the same spirit, by the spirit of God. The personage seen coming in the clouds of heaven by Daniel in his first vision, is the same seen by the Revelator in the 7th verse of the same chapter, in which he saw the personage in the midst of the seven golden candlesticks. Each saw the cloud come before they saw the personage. Daniel says it was for a long time.

Then the angel came to Daniel again, saying, "Now I am come to make thee understand what shall befall thy people in the latter days, for yet the vision is for many days." These days are years, mark, 14th verse. Again, 20th and 21st verses. "Then said he, knowest thou wherefore I am come unto thee? and now I will return to fight with the prince of Persia, and when I am gone forth, lo, the prince of Grecia shall come. But I will show thee that which is noted in the Scriptures of Truth, and there is none that holdeth with me in these things but the other the Son, in the spirit-world. Hence Michael comes in now as your humble servant's prince, the prince of second Daniel; and hence his doctrine is the only true doctrine on earth. It throws Spiritualism in the shade, with all other doctrines, knowing of the truth of the Scriptures, or of coming events.

We now proceed to the 11th chapter, in which the angel gives a more extended account of all matters in the visions. I will transcribe a few verses: "Also I in the first year of Darius the Mede, even I, stood to confirm and to strengthen him. And now will I show thee the truth. Behold, there shall stand up three kings in Persia, and the fourth shall be far richer than they all, and by his strength through his riches he shall stir up all against the realm of Grecia. And a mighty king shall stand up that shall rule with great dominion, and do according to his will. And when he shall stand up his kingdom shall be broken, and be divided toward the four winds of heaven, and not for his posterity, nor according to his dominion which he ruled, for his kingdom shall be plucked up, even for others beside those." Thus reads the first four verses.

Here the reader must keep in mind that the angel stood to confirm and strengthen Daniel in the first year of Darius the Mede. This was the Darius which took the kingdom of Belshazzar, as in Daniel 5, 31, when the golden head, or in other words, the beast's head, all the then known world had been given to the Medes and Persians. When king Cyrus came to the throne, he said that God had given him all the kingdoms of the earth, as in the last verse of 2d Book of Chron., and in the Book of Ezra, 1st chapter, 2d verse. This was brought about by the union of the Mede and Persian kingdom by a marriage, which gave king Cyrus all the then known world, all the kingdoms which composed all the then known world; and in the third year of his reign Daniel had this vision, at the close of which the angel makes known to him the truth in regard to these matters.

He says there shall yet stand up three kings in Persia—that is three besides king Cyrus. And the fourth shall be far richer than they all. This fourth king was the king of Grecia. The same the angel refers to in the 2d verse of the 10th chapter, as coming whilst he returned to fight with the prince of Persia. This king, with his strength and riches, should stir up all the realm against him—against Grecia. When a mighty king should stand up and rule with great dominion. This was the king of Rome, who conquered the Greeks. And when he should stand up his kingdom should be broken, and divided to the four winds of heaven, and not to his posterity. This was the case with the king that conquered the Greeks. He had no heir to his throne, when he divided his dominions between his four Generals, which passed it as to the four winds of the heaven, dividing it into four parts. For his kingdom shall be plucked up for others besides those. This was represented when Pagan Rome fell into ten kingdoms, it was plucked up for others besides those—beside those four kings.

Now, before going any farther, I will trace this matter, showing you the four heads of the dragon. You must keep in mind when Nebuchadnezzar became a beast, the spirit of the woman was in the beast, the woman was in the devil, not as dead ghost, but as live ghost. The meaning is that the spirit of God is trampled under foot by the devil. The Medo-Persians conquering the Babylonean monarchy, represented the trampling of God in Abraham under foot, this gave the Medes and Persians Great Babylon—all the then known world. The Greeks conquering the Medes and Persians, trampled Isaac and Rebecca in the spirit of God under foot, which gave the Greeks Great Babylon—all the then known world. The Romans conquering the Greeks, trampled Esau in the spirit of God under foot, which gave the Romans Great Babylon—all the then known world. Now, mark, the spirit of Jacob, live ghost for God's kingdom, stood in Pagan Rome in the devil. Here Esau stands third in these conquests, consequently he stands as ghost for the devil. Had Esau not been born as live ghost for the devil, there could have been no Greek nation as ghost for Jacob to have conquered in the devil.

Again: Pagan Rome being divided between four kings, represents Jacob's four sons—Reuben, Simeon, Levi, and Judah. These kingdoms eventually revert back again into one, and stand in the spirit of Judah in the devil, until they fall into ten kingdoms, which represents Jacob and his other nine children, the whole having been represented in the devil. Abraham, Isaac, Esau, Jacob and his thirteen children, all in kingdoms in the spirit of the devil.

Again: I will now show you how the four heads were made. Nebuchadnezzar was the beast. The Medo-Persians conquered the beast and jump astride of him—astride of that power. Then the beast had two heads. The Greeks conquer the Medo-Persians, when they jump astride of the beast—then the beast had three heads. The Romans conquer the Greeks, when they jump astride of the beast—then the beast had four heads. Now, we will suppose a crown of four heads is made for Pagan Rome. The spirit of this crown remains in Pagan Rome, and when she falls into ten kingdoms it remains in Rome in the spirit of Jacob in the devil.

Again: The Greek's mark was the goat's head out of which the four horns came, out of one of which came the little horn. Keep in mind now that this head, as well as all the others, embraced all the then known world. Rome came in possession of the goat's head by conquest, when out of the goat's head comes the four kingdoms which represent the image, viz: Papal Rome, Spain, France, and England. The seat of Pagan Rome was transferred to Papal Rome in the year six hundred and six, when Papal Rome receives the crown of four heads. Keep these things in mind.

These four kingdoms are the same set in type by the four horns which came up out of the goat's head, which was set in type by the four beasts seen in Daniel's first vision. Papal Rome is the lion, Spain is the bear, which had three ribs in his mouth, and power to destroy much flesh. Keep in mind the Inquisition was established in Spain, where much flesh was destroyed. France is the leopard which had four wings as of a fowl, and four heads. I will show how she gets these four heads after a while. England is the beast with ten horns, and the little horn. Here you must keep in mind that England, in six hundred and six of the Christian era, did not possess the two islands she does now. At that time, what is now England, possessed ten Kingdoms, or soon after that time, therefore the image was not represented in the four Kingdoms at that time, but is now, as I shall soon show.

You will now see that Jacob's children are again all represented in the image, in Papal Rome. The Spirit being transferred from Pagan Rome to Papal Rome, transfers the Spirit in the Devil, from Jacob to Reuben, his first born son. This places the father in the son, anti-God or Devil, which you please. Spain stands in the spirit of Simeon, France in the spirit of Levi, and England in the spirit of Judah, and the seven Saxon kingdoms added to Reuben, Simeon and Levi, makes ten, to which add the kingdom of Scotland, the kingdom of Ireland, and the kingdom of

Wales, and you have just thirteen. These are some of the wonders of God's wisdom. And when you add to this the fact that the very soil of England was divided to represent Jacob's two wives, and two concubines, and also Jacob himself, it places the wisdom of God beyond the comprehension of men. Britain represented Leah, and Ireland her maid; Scotland Rachael, and Wales her maid, whilst the Isle of Man represented Jacob between his four wives. Now you have got the plain facts of the case, as I shall prove most conclusively from this out.

Now, having found Daniel's beast with ten horns, we will see if we can find the little horn. In this connection you must keep in mind that kings represent those horns. In the tenth or eleventh century William the conqueror spread his pavilion over the seven Saxon kingdoms of England, in the spirit of Jacob's daughter, who was born eleven in turn of birth with the other children. The ten sons born previous to her are represented in the ten Kings, and she, being eleventh, comes in in William the Conqueror; hence the spirit of the woman is the conqueror. The throne of England from that time up, stands in the spirit of the woman. This throne then proceeds to conquer the kings of Scotland, Ireland and Wales, and uniting them to England, thus plucking up three of the ten horns, by the roots, completely fulfilling the prophecy of Daniel. I suppose you will still say in the face of all this that men are free agents. Well, have it so then.

As stated in the Bridegroom, England received God's kingdom in the union of Scotland with England, by a marriage, notwithstanding its having been conquered. This originates from the fact that Scotland stood in the spirit of Rachael, who was the type of the spiritual Kingdom of God, and as Jacob received Rachael last, so she in spirit must come into England by marriage. Wales, which stood in the spirit of her maid, partook of the spirit of Rachael, and therefore had to be united to England by an additional tenure to conquest, by which the heirs to the throne receives the name of Prince of Wales. This is at least the case with the kings of the throne of England. Ireland, being Leah's hand-maid, and she being the type of the natural kingdom of God, had to be held by conquest alone, thus, first natural, and afterward spiritual, as Paul says.

England, receiving God's Kingdom in King James the First, represents the clay in the feet of the image. The Jewish kingdom having started from Abraham, who was called to replace the first Adam who was made of clay, constitutes the clay in the feet of the image. This was again represented in Scotland by a different worship, a worship called Protestantism. The different kinds of metal in the image were only to designate for different kingdoms, the whole designed as a type of image worship, whilst the clay in them was a type of a different.

Almost the first thing done by King James was to lay off the east coast of the new world into two districts, upon which settled twelve Colonies in the spirit of twelve of Jacob's children. The thirteenth Colony was settled to represent the birth of Benjamin, who was the last child born, as will be shown in the chapter on the Jewish kingdom. These Colonies constituted the toes of the image. They were born into a kingdom of twelve thrones, but only a ghost kingdom, a President without a crown. It is not termed a kingdom by Daniel; only the dividing of the fourth kingdom, as in Daniel 2 : 41, as follows: " And whereas thou sawest the feet and toes, part of potter's clay and part of iron, the kingdom shall be divided, but there shall be in it the strength of the iron, forasmuch as thou sawest the iron mixed with miry clay."

Thus you will see that Daniel don't consider this a kingdom as yet, only the dividing of the kingdom with ten horns, and the little horn. The Union must now go on until the thirteen Apostles who represent the thirteen children of Jacob have been represented in the Presidency, this closed with Buchanan's reign, which brings us in the very days of the kings who rule in the four kingdoms that represent the image, and before Abraham leaves the throne of the twelve-throne kingdom, the God of Heaven will be here and set up the kingdom in the days of these kings, precisely as Daniel stated. I shall now halt with Buchanan until I bring up many other things.

I will first direct the attention of Dr. Pitts, and all other wise men, to the feet and toes of the image, by asking them if the two Islands of England do not look more like the two feet of such an image than Pagan Rome? It seems to me that no man can be so blind but that he can see this, more especially after it is pointed out to him. Again, does not the colonies look more like the toes of such an image, than the ten kingdoms into which Pagan Rome fell. This, I think, everybody must admit. The reader might here say that the thirteen do not represent ten. True, but mark, one of the thirteen belongs in the midst of the twelve, and this was settled entirely outside of the two districts. Again, you will find by consulting history, that the two districts over-lap each other in the middle, which God had done on purpose to represent the toes. Now I hope these things are plain.

I will now prepare your mind for the reception of the other three heads of the dragon. You must here keep in mind, as shown above, that God, in spirit, brought Adam and Eve on this side of Cain and the dead ghost. These are now represented in the four kingdoms that represent the Image; Rome stands in the spirit of Cain; Spain in the spirit of the Dead Ghost; France in the spirit of Adam; and England in the spirit of Eve; thus doubly representing the four kingdoms. The Pope standing in the spirit of Cain, who had the spirit of the woman represented in Abel dead in him. The Pope and Priests could have no wives, at least lawful ones; hence the Pope must have a spiritual wife, which was represented in England as Eve; Rome, Spain and France, representing the Pope in the Trinity as anti-god. Henry the Eighth of England has England divorced from Rome, from the Pope. The people of England make him Pope of the Church of England; thus England, the wife of the dragon, gives birth to a son for the old *fellow*. This Henry is the beast with seven heads, ten horns, and ten crowns upon the horns. Rev. 13: 1. The spirit of the seven Saxon princes in the throne constitute the type of the seven heads of the beast. These heads were represented by the seven Henrys that preceded Henry the Eighth, the first one having been an usurper of the throne. This, you see, places Rome, Spain and France, as the Father, and England the Son, and this Union, born from England, as the Ghost, all in anti-god, all in the devil.

We will now go back to Nebuchadnezzar, the beast, and trace down the seven heads of the beast. The Medo-Persians conquer, and jump astride of the beast, when it has two heads. The Greeks conquer it, and jump astride, when it has three heads. The Romans conquer the Greeks, and jump astride, when the beast has four heads. This closes the great conquests. Now, a crown is made for the beast of four heads. This crown is transferred from Pagan Rome to Papal Rome, in the year six hundred and six. This locks the dragon in the bottomless pit as in Rev. 21: 1, 2, 3. The old world is the bottomless pit; everything established on it must disappear as would anything cast into a pit without a bottom. He being chained in the pit, cannot make any heads for himself. Spain being the ghost, dead in the Pope, she cannot make any heads. France, standing in the spirit of Adam, she must make a head to represent Adam. Thus old Napoleon springs up after the thousand years expire, when he calls upon the Pope to come and crown him Emperor of France; he refuses to do it. Old Napoleon proceeds to Rome with his army and encamps outside the city, and with a few of his aids, proceeded to the palace of the Pope, where he finds him sitting on his Chair of State. He walks up against the chair, throwing it over and spilling the Pope out on the floor, then steps over him, and turns around, takes the crown off the Pope's head, puts it upon his own and marches off with it. This unlocks the bottomless pit and lets the spirit of the beast, the spirit of the devil, out. Napoleon jumps astride of the beast and runs his career, when the beast has five heads. He stumbles against England, when he is conquered, and England jumps astride of the beast, and is making the sixth head for the dragon, which is the head of Eve. Louis Napoleon must now conquer England in order to jump astride of the beast and make the seventh and last head. Keep these things in mind.

We will now see how this agrees with the Revelator. In the 17th chapter, is the account of the scarlet-colored beast with seven heads and ten horns. The angel, explaining this beast with seven heads and ten horns, says, "The seven heads are seven mountains on which the woman sitteth." These seven mountains are the seven hills on which the city of Rome sits. (I will explain fully about this woman in the chapter on the Revelation, which is the next chapter in the work. My object here is to point out the heads of the dragon.) "And there are seven kings, one for each mountain. Five are fallen; one is, the other is not yet come, and when he cometh he must abide a short space. And the beast that was, and is not, even he is the eighth, but of the seven, of the spirit of Nebuchadnezzar, the beast, and he goeth into perdition. 9th, 10th, and 11th verses. Now we will see how this agrees with the above. Five are fallen. Keep in mind that old Napoleon made the fifth head, hence he was the fifth king. The kings, of Babylon, Medo-Persian, Grecian, and Roman, being the other four, the five now being dead, fallen. Her Majesty, Queen Victoria, is now riding the beast that is making the sixth head. England is making the sixth head for the dragon, and the Queen represents the woman here riding the beast, as the one that is, as in the 10th verse, five fallen and one is. And Louis Napoleon is the one not yet come, and when he cometh, he must abide a short space, and the beast is the eighth, but of the seven, of the same spirit. Thus you will see perfect harmony throughout.

The reader will, no doubt, say why can't some other king make this last head as well as Louis Napoleon? Answer—Because the last head is the Old Serpent's Head, the same which beguiled Mother Eve, or rather that made her a mother. This was the lower head in Adam; and as France stands in the spirit of Adam, she must make two heads. Old Napoleon made a head for the upper one, and Louis Napoleon must make a head for the lower one. France also is the third kingdom in the image, and the image being that of a man, the head is in that part of the image which France represents. You will therefore see that it is not possible for any other man on earth to make that head but Louis Napoleon.

Again: You will see that these heads are represented first last. Adam and Eve were first; Abraham, Isaac, Esau, and Jacob, last. Now, mark,

Abraham, Isaac, Esau, and Jacob, were represented in Babylon; Medo-Persian, Greeks and Roman, in the devil. And now comes Adam, Eve, and the Serpents, last. This last head being the serpent's head, the representation will be the most awful ever taken place on earth. Slaughter, rapine, murder, massacre, and everything else, will accompany it. This calamity has now commenced in this Union (Mark 13, 14,) which will be fully proven before I get through.

We will now go back and see how the prophecy of Daniel agrees with this. We left off at the close of the 4th verse of the 11th chapter, which, as stated above, gave us the close of Pagan Rome by falling into ten kingdoms. By reading a portion of that chapter, as far as the thirteenth verse, you will see the meanderings of different kings with their armies, in very short hand. The 13th verse reads thus: "For the King of the North shall return, and shall set forth a multitude greater than the former, and shall certainly come after certain years with a great army and much riches." This Kingdom of the North is England, in the spirit of the little horn. And in those times there shall many stand up against the King of the South, also the rulers of thy people shall exalt themselves to establish the vision, but they shall fail. 14th verse.—This verse shows a great struggle between the king of the North and the king of the South. France is this king of the South. The rulers of Daniel's people were trying to bring the vision about. Rome stood in the spirit of the robbers of Daniel's people; Papal Rome received the spirit of Pagan Rome, who robbed and destroyed the Jewish people, who were Daniel's people. But as France was the acting power for Rome it was France against England trying to bring about the vision. 15th verse—So the king of the North shall come and cast up a mount, and take the most fenced cities, and the arms of the South shall not withstand, neither shall his chosen people, neither shall their be any strength to withstand. This shows that neither of those parties should accomplish anything at that time. 16th verse—But him that cometh against him shall do according to his own will, and none shall stand before him, and he shall stand in the glorious land which by his hand shall be consumed. This personage was old Bonaparte. The glorious land means the Land of Canaan, the Holy Land, in which old Bonaparte camped his army. 17th verse—He shall also set his face to enter with his whole kingdom, and upright ones with him; thus shall he do, and he shall give him the daughter of woman, corrupting her; but she shall not stand on his side, neither be for him. This verse has the spirit of Bonaparte's divorce from Josephine. A daughter of another woman was given him for a wife, she was not for him. Josephine was his star, and when he lost her he lost the spirit. I will show you in the next chapter why this had to be done. His second wife did not give him the spirit, hence Daniel says she was not for him. I said Daniel, but I should have said the angel, as the angel is telling Daniel all this. This verse also contains the type of his failure at Moscow. 18th and 19th verses—After this shall he turn his face unto the isles, and shall take many, and a prince for his own behalf shall cause the reproach offered by him to cease, without his own reproach he shall cause it to turn upon him. Then he shall turn his face toward the fort of his own land, but he shall stumble and fall, and not be found. This was his return from Mocsow, and his last battle with England, when the beast stumbled and fell, throwing him off, when England jumped astride of the beast, and old Bonaparte was not found on the throne of France—thus completely fulfilling the above, which will be made still plainer.

This also fulfills what I stated above about old Bonaparte being the great king mentioned at the close of the 8th chapter, the vision of the ram and goat as the man which should arise up in the latter time of the four kingdoms, set in type by the four horns which came up out of the goat's head. Old Napoleon was of fierce countenance, and understood dark sentences, and ruled with a power not his own. No, his power was in Josephine, and when he put her away his power was gone. Truly mankind are but machines in God's hand. Now, keep in mind that France was the third kingdom in the image, and that old Napoleon took the crown of four heads off the Pope's head and put it on his own—when you have Daniel's third beast with four heads, and four wings as of a fowl. Wings implies speed, that was represented by Napoleon in the marching of his army. He was always upon his enemy three or four days before he looked for him. Again: The four kingdoms was in their latter days in his lifetime, as the angel says in 8th chapter, 23d verse, that this king should rise up in the latter time of their kingdom, when the transgressors had came to the full. Fifty years have passed since his days, hence the end of those kingdoms must now be very close at hand, which will now be further shown.

We will now continue on the 20th verse—Then shall stand up in his estate a raiser of taxes in the glory of the kingdom, but within few days he shall be destroyed, neither in anger nor in battle. This personage was Louis Phillippe He took the throne of France a poor man, and left it one of the richest men in the world, showing himself to be the man the angel sent then to make the letter to the type. These days means years. He was destroyed, but neither in battle nor anger.

21st verse—And in his estate shall stand up a vile person, to whom they shall not give the honor of the kingdom, but he shall come in peaceably, and obtain the kingdom by flatteries. This personage is the present Louis Napoleon. The angel calls him a vile person. He obtained the kingdom by flatteries, just as stated; everything corroborating every word of the angel.

22d and 23d verses—And with the arms of a flood shall they be overflown from before him, and shall be broken, yea, also the prince of the Covenant. And after the league made with him, he shall work deceitfully, for he shall come up and become strong with a small people. This league set in type in Daniel's first vision. He says the fourth beast has iron teeth (7th chapter, 7th verse); and in the 7th chapter and 19th verse, it has iron teeth and brass nails—a league between the iron and brass kingdoms. This is the alliance now existing between England and France—the iron and brass kingdoms in the image. The angel says he shall work deceitfully. This he will do just so sure as the angel said so. They have been overflown from before him at both Russia and Austria. Most certainly no one can be so blind as to read this and not see the fulfillment of these things taking place yearly. Furthermore, he shall grow up and become strong with a small people. This I will show before I close.

24th verse. He shall enter peaceably upon the fattest places of the province, and he shall do that which his fathers have not done, nor his father's fathers. He shall scatter among them the prey, and spoils, and riches, yea, he shall cast his devices against the strongholds, even for a time. This you will see he has in part already done. He has entered peaceably, as it were, the fattest places of the provinces, in his taking of Mexico. I will point out the spoils before I close. He shall cast his devices against the strongholds. This, I will show, will be his conquering of England, which will be fully accomplished by the time he arrives at the announcement of the 31st verse. And arms shall stand on his part and they shall pollute the sanctuary of strength, and shall take away the daily sacrifice, and they shall place the abomination that maketh desolate. This will be the conquering of England, and the same referred to by what Daniel overheard the Saints talking about, in 8th ch., 13th vs·, the verse proceeding the twenty-three hundred days. Read this chapter out and you will find this vile person is the combattant, and the one side to the end of the chapter, of which many points will be noticed before I close.

The time of setting up this abomination is set by the Revelator, in 11th chap. 1st, 2nd verse : "And there was given me a reed like unto a rod, and the Angel stood, saying : rise and measure the temple of God, and the altar, and them that worship therein. But the court which is without the temple leave out, and measure it not, for it is given unto the Gentiles, and the holy city shall they tread under foot forty and two months." This measurement commenced with the crowning of the first Pope, in the year 606. Mark, as stated above, the court connected with the tabernacle was a type of the dragon's kingdom, which was given to the Gentiles, in the Pope, transferred from Pagan Rome. It was not measured. The tabernacle became the temple built by Solomon, and is represented in England, hence England was the temple measured for forty and two months. Forty and two prophetic months would make twelve hundred and three score prophetic days, and a prophetic day being a year with us, would make twelve hundred and three score years from the time the measurement took place. Now commence with the year 606 and add to them 1860 years, and you will close with the year 1866. The measuring of England was only to keep her from being conquered until that time. You will see that during this forty and two months the holy city is to be trodden under foot. It was called the holy city from the fact that it was to receive God's kingdom, of which the holy place in the Tabernacle was a type, and now stands as the holy place in the Tabernacle. Hence the abomination of desolation is to be set up by Louis Napoleon, when Jesus will redeem it and cleanse the Sanctuary, as in Daniel 8: 14. Hence this conquest of England must take place before the close of the year 1866.

I will now notice one item more in connection with Daniel's four beasts, and then pass on to notice Nebuchadnezzar, the tree. Daniel saw in his night vision, those four beasts rise up out of the sea, one diverse from another. You must keep in mind that the sea mentioned here is not the Ocean, but the Catholic See. The type of this Catholic See was set in the sea Solomon had made for the temple, as in 1st Kings, 8th ch. 23d to 25th verse. This See was placed in the temple, or porch, as the emblem of the flood that drowned the antedeluvian world. This See Pagan Rome stole from God's house, when they destroyed the temple at old Jerusalem, as well as the candlestick with six branches, together with all the manuscripts of the Bible, and furniture of the House, including the mercy seat. This was all transfered to Papal Rome when it became the furniture of the devil's house. This sea then became the Papal See, out of which Daniel saw these four beasts rise : Rome, Spain, France and England, and are the very Kingdoms that represent the image. These are the only four kingdoms ever having existed on earth to which one man gave law and gospel ; the only four kingdoms ever having been ruled by one man. For a term of more than three hundred years did the Pope put up Kings, and set the basest of men upon thrones in these four kingdoms, as anti-God, shadowed forth in Daniel 4 : 17. This shows most conclusively, that these kingdoms were connected together to represent the image in its four parts, as are those four parts of a man connected. As the head of a man rules those four parts, so have those four kingdoms been ruled by one man.

I will now notice an item just received which stands in connection with a passage noted above, 11th chapter, 14th verse, where the robbers of Daniel's people should try to establish the vision. Jesus tells us in John 10: 1, "Verily, verily, I say unto you, he that entereth not by the door of the sheepfold, but climbeth up some other way, the same is a thief and robber." The Jewish kingdom is the sheepfold here referred to. When Pagan Rome entered the sheepfold, she did not enter the door, or gate of the city. No, she battered the wall down and climbed up outside, and therefore stands as the thief and robber, as stated above. Hence, when this spirit was transferred to Papal Rome, father in the son, she stands as the thief and robber, represented in the Trinity, in Rome, Spain and France.

Now, the question is, how did the robbers of Daniel's people try to bring the vision about? I will tell you. You will recollect that history tells us that Spain attempted to conquer England in the latter part of the fifteenth century, I think. This attempt was called the Spanish Armada. God sent a storm that destroyed the fleet, and the project failed, just as the angel said it should. You will see by this that the establishing of the vision, must be the conquering of England. This, you see, took place before old Napoleon's day, more than a hundred years before, hence stands in this chapter before the coming in of Napoleon, as above. This is in the 14th verse, and old Napoleon comes in in the 16th, and stumbles and falls, and is not found in the 19th verse—not found upon the throne of France. Again, not far from this time, the Saint Bartholomew massacre took place in France, when seventy thousand Protestants were massacred. This was also an attempt to bring about the vision, but it failed also. This implies a great massacre through the world, about the time this abomination of desolation is set up by Louis Napoleon, which will be proven more abundantly in the further progress of this work.

We will now proceed to notice Nebuchadnezzar as the Tree. I must here again go back to the first Adam. In the Bridegroom I proved to you that Adam was in the figure of an oak tree, and Eve in him. He was placed in the garden of the Lord, when Eve was taken out of him. When God met Abram in the plains of Mamre, he met him in the Trinity in three men, or angels, Gen. 18: 1, 5. This meeting took place under a tree. The account does not say under an oak tree, but a tree. Under this tree Isaac was promised, as in 10th verse. Now mark, Abram was called to replace the first Adam at the head of God's kingdom; his name was changed as well as that of his wife, which raises them a degree higher in the scale of civilization. This places God's natural kingdom, which was in the figure of an oak tree, under a tree. The spirit of all this was in the kingdom when given to Nebuchadnezzar in the golden head of the image, after which he became a Great Tree that reached up to heaven, and the sight thereof unto the ends of the earth.

Now here keep in mind that this tree is connected with the image, and that the tree is a spiritual one, as was the image a spiritual one, represented in four kingdoms, and that this tree does not commence its spiritual growth until the image commences its growth. This was in the year 606, which places the tree beside the image; and as England is the feet of the image, the tree stands beside the feet, hence on the opposite side of the channel from England. This tree was the type of image worship outside of the image, extending to the ends of the earth, but not in the same form as in the four kingdoms. In the four kingdoms, the worship was ruled by one man in Church and State; but in the tree this man did not rule in State, only in Church. Hence the churches outside of the image are connected with the Pope, similar to the branches being connected with a tree. This is the reason why the dream of the tree followed the dream of the image with Nebuchadnezzar, so the worship of images had to spread outside the image to the ends of the earth. Had it not been for this, image-worship could not have extended beyond the four kingdoms. The four kinds of metal in the image was only to designate four kingdoms, and to show the time when the feet and toes was fully represented.

Again. From the time the spirit was transferred from Pagan Rome to Papal Rome, this tree has been growing, and was the spiritual representative of the tree under which God met Abram, and under which Isaac was promised, who was born according to the spirit of promise, and was the first white child ever born, who was a type of Jesus. Hence God's kingdom, or the spirit of it, was trampled under foot under this spiritual tree, until the last battle fought between England and France. England and France being the iron and brass kingdoms in the image, cut down that tree in the battle of Waterloo, and left an iron and brass band on the stump of the tree in the tender grass of the field. This battle took place on the opposite side of the channel, on German soil, I believe. The iron is first mentioned in the band, a type that the iron kingdom would gain the victory. Now you all know that England, the iron kingdom in the image, did gain that victory, proving positively that God over-ruled the armies.

Again. The very moment that the spiritual tree was cut down with God's spiritual war-ax, old Napoleon's army ran, proving most conclusively that Popery stands in the spirit of the beast, Nebuchadnezzar. Beasts run, but trees cannot. This left the dragon as the beast, and England as the Oak Tree. From the time the tree was cut down, Popery has been on the decrease in the Old World. Could it have been otherwise, had France gained the victory, Popery would still have been in its glory. But God's plan must be carried out, let the result be what it may.

Again. Keep in mind that the same old Napoleon is the great king which Daniel, or in other words, which the angel told Daniel, should arise up in the latter time of their kingdom, understanding dark sentences, and that he made the fifth head for the dragon. In the chapter on the Revelation, I will show you his career in Moscow, which will still make matters more plain. You can now account for the watcher that came down from heaven, and said, "Cut the tree down." This watcher was the Angel Gabriel, who overruled the armies so as to cut the tree down.

Now, in this connection, you must keep in mind, that, as the United States is only the division of England and not a kingdom, no crown worn in it, and as it is the toes of the image, and in the New World, it must have a tree to represent Nebuchadnezzar's tree. This tree is the Liberty Tree, the liberty pole, a tree cut from the stump and transplanted. This Union was born from England before Nebuchadnezzar's tree was cut down. This liberty tree was cut down in the Bull Run battle, and the very moment it was cut down with the spiritual battle-ax, the Union

army ran. This shows where the spirit of the beast stands. The Union,
under Abraham, stands in the spirit of the dragon, and Abraham and
his Cabinet represent the beast with seven heads. The first State that
seceded had a tree on its flag, which represents the tree under which
God met Abram in the Trinity, and under it Isaac, who was a type of Jesus,
was promised. Jesus being Isaac's representative, must be here before
Abraham leaves the Presidential chair, when God will be in the Trinity in
Jesus, when he will meet Abraham under that tree, or meet the sceptre
of Abraham under the tree. Now these are matters of fact, such as the
wisdom of the world cannot gainsay. God says, "my ways are not your
ways, neither are my thoughts your thoughts."

I will now notice another item connected with Nebuchadnezzar's tree.
Mark, as stated above, the spirit of the woman passed from the head of
the woman, as implied in the bonnets made for Aaron, into the head of
Aaron. At the same time they made breeches for him to hide his naked-
ness—Ex. 28 : 42. These breeches reached all the way from the loins to
the thighs, a length at most, of nine inches. It was this spirit of the
woman that made Nebuchadnezzar the golden head of the image, and
that made his tree grow to Heaven, and the sight thereof to the ends of
the earth. Here you must keep in mind the Heaven referred to was
this Union, as the Revelator saw descend out of Heaven from God, as
proven in the Bridegroom. When the tree was cut down by England
and France, the spirit left the man and returned to the woman again,
where they stand as the stump of the tree. And when Louis Napoleon
takes the throne of France, he takes a wife, who puts the iron and brass
band around the stump of the tree, by putting the hoops around the women. The women now stand as the stump of the tree, with an iron and
brass band. This spirit, you see, comes from the beast, from Bonaparte's
side of the house.

Now keep in mind that prior to cutting the tree down, the men of
England wore the breeches set in type, by the breeches made for Aaron.
From the time that the tree was cut down, the breeches have been grad-
ually leaving the men of England, and creeping upon the women of the
world. Whilst now the women stand under the hat, and in the coat, in
the hoops, and in the breeches, and in the spirit of the Serpent which
was hid by the breeches made for Aaron. This serpent was similar to
the one that beguiled mother Eve, and there can be no doubt that a similar serpent will beguile many of these women who manifest this spirit
by lifting their skirts so high when they walk out, or those who drag
those long trains, or trails after them. Mark, a serpent trails himself on
the ground. I don't utter these things because I find fault with them;
no, but because to show you that God, in the spirit of the devil, makes
you do it. I should never find fault in a woman pulling up her skirts,
for there is nothing that I like to see better than a woman's leg. But I
do dislike to see those dirty, filthy trains. Had it not been for those
hoops and trains, not half of the number of women would have perished
in the recent conflagration in the capitol of Chili, in South America.
But as the dragon is in the spirit of this serpent, the hoops and trains
must do their work. It would be useless for me to say, cast them from
you as you would a viper, for I know you can't do it until God makes
you. I also know that that time is close at hand. Yes, when he meets
Abraham under the tree, then they will be hurled away as vipers.

Now, before I proceed to make the connections I must pay a passing
notice to the charter in the Oak tree. I have been charged with making
a misstatement. This I may be as likely to do as anybody else quoting

from history. I am told that it was the Charter of Connecticut that was hid in the Oak tree, instead of that of Rhode Island, as stated in the Bridegroom. In examining history I find it the case. I quoted that from memory, not having read that for several years. · But let me ask, what difference does it make whether the Charter of Rhode Island or that of any other State was in the Oak. I only pointed to the fact to show that the Colonies, as well as the Union, stood as Eve in Adam. I now see that the error is only calculated to make the matter more plain and forcible. Both Charters were resumed after Mary and William took the throne of England. It does not say whether the Rhode Island Charter was in the Oak or not, but the Connecticut Charter was. Connecticut stood in the spirit of Adam, and Rhode Island in that of Eve. The Charter of Connecticut was the spirit of woman, and that being in the Oak, implies Eve in Adam for the Colonies and the Government of Payton Randolph. Rhode Island being admitted into the Union on that Charter, places the throne of the Union in the spirit of Adam, with Eve in him. Thus you see that it is plainer and more feasible than before. As stated in the Bridegroom, the Prince of Wales planting the Oak tree in the Central Park of New York, placed Adam in the garden of the Lord. I will now add to that, as he also planted an acorn at the grave of Washington, it placed the Union in the spirit of Adam and Eve. The new Union coming out of the old Union, placed the Union in the spirit of Eve and Adam. The Democrat party of the old Union represented Adam, from the day of its birth, whilst the spirit of the new Union stands in the women of the South, which will be proven as I proceed. Before doing so I must say a few words more on the Union, as Eve in Adam.

In all Kingdoms a Queen gives birth to an heir for the throne, but as the Union is not a kingdom, there is no Queen to give birth to the heir of the Presidential chair. This is the reason why men must give birth to an heir for the chair. Hence, men does the woman's work. Men have to be man and woman, both—Eve in Adam. Men elect a President and this gives birth to an heir to the chair for four years. Again, why must there have been one elected every four years; why not every ten? Because, every fourth year is leap year, the woman's year; hence, an election for President must take place every fourth year. The men must be women every fourth year. This is God's reason for having the President elected on leap year, because the throne belongs to Jesus, the seed of the woman. Now, if you want any more evidence that the Union stood Eve in Adam, then just wait a few months until God comes, and He will give it to you.

I shall now proceed to make the connections, and before doing so must refer you to what I stated in the Bridegroom, viz: That certain men, women and children, as well as beasts and horses, were types, and when the letters are made to those types, certain men and women represent them in power, in thrones; as, for instance, England is Daniel's Beast, with the horns united into one kingdom, and stands in the spirit of the little horn, and now represented by Her Majesty Queen Victoria. These horns had previously been represented by men as kings. The Apostles were represented by the States in the union, and thus the types are lettered. In making these different connections, you will see that certain men and women represent a number of types, represent several different persons having lived in different ages of the world. Now, with this explanation I shall proceed :

Eve was taken out of Adam in the Garden of the Lord, as in Gen. 2d chapter. The Garden of the Lord was eastward in Eden. Gen. 2, 8: 9th verse. From this forward Eve was the golden head. This spirit in God's kingdom made Nebuchadnezzar the golden head, and when a beast this spirit was trodden under foot, and comes out in England with Queen Victoria, the golden head on the throne. This Union born from England, but, as Daniel has it, only the division of England, it stands in the spirit of Adam, the golden head, as Eve in him. This new throne coming out of the old one is Eve taken out of Adam in the Garden of the Lord, and stands in the spirit of the golden head the women of the South. This places the Union in the spirit of the Land of Eden, and the Southern States as the Garden of the Lord eastward in Eden. This is palpably true when you take into consideration that the Union extends to the Pacific Coast, and the Southern States do not extend half way. This places the Northern States in the spirit of Adam, governed by the Democratic party, and Eve in the Southern States.

Again : The powers that have taken the place of the Democratic power say they will restore the old Union by putting the South back into it again. In answer to this I have only to say what I have always said since the difficulty commenced—if you can find any evidence in the Bible showing you that Eve was put back into Adam again, then you have some evidence that you can put the South back into the Union again. But as there is no evidence of this character to be found in the Bible, I now say to you that all the armies on the face of the earth cannot accomplish the feat.

Again : The powers that be say if they cannot restore the Union they will kill the South, or exterminate it. Now, I say as I have always said, if you can find any evidence in the Bible that Adam killed Eve, or exterminated her, then you can have some hopes of accomplishing the great feat undertaken. But as no such evidence is to be found in the Bible, I can only say as above, that had you all the armies of the world you would fail in accomplishing the task. If you kill every man in the Southern Confederacy you do not affect in the least the spirit of the throne inasmuch as it stands in the woman.

Again : I proved, too, in the Bridegroom that Eve was the soul of Adam, and when Eve was taken out of him he had no soul. Just so with this Union, until the close of Buchanan's reign, or in other words until Abraham's election, the soul was in the Union; the very moment the new throne came out of the old one it had no soul. And as Eve supplied the souls of all men, so this new throne must be the soul of all thrones on earth, and will be supplied them by God admitting them into this soul, the germ of his throne.

We will now notice another class of connections. Cain and Abel were begotten by Adam—Cain to represent Adam, and Abel to represent Eve. Abraham is the representative of Cain, whilst Davis is the representative of Abel. Here the reader may object and say the Democratic party did not elect Abraham. To this I say that they did, for had none of them voted for him he would not have been elected. This makes the Democratic party which stands as Adam, natural God, the father of Abraham, the father of Cain. And Davis in his power came out of the old Union, which stood in the spirit of Adam, and therefore represents Abel. Thus you see that this is all right; Cain is representing Adam, whilst Abel is representing Eve. Cain fighting for Adam and Abel fighting for Eve. You must now keep in mind that the two powers represent the two men, headed by Abraham and Davis.

Again : Cain killed Abel because Abel's offering had been accepted by God. Now, Abraham must kill Davis, or kill his power. But mark, Cain killing Abel did not affect Eve; so when Abraham kills the power of Davis it will not affect Eve in the women. Again : Jesus says " ye do not understand my speech, even because ye cannot hear my word. Ye are of your father the devil, and the lust of your father ye will do. He was a murderer from the beginning, and abode not in the truth, because there was no truth in him. When he speaketh a lie he speaketh of his own, for he is a liar and the father of it." John, 8 : 43, 44. This language makes the first murderer the devil, and everybody who believes the Bible believes that Cain was a murderer from the beginning, and a liar and the father of it. This places Abraham and his power in the spirit of the devil. He also represents the murderer, and the liar, and the father of lies. Now, keep in mind that this all stands in the power. Abraham is a good man enough, speaking after the manner of man, but the spirit that overrules him places him in this position.

Again : As the language above was uttered by Jesus, who had also been first Adam, we will notice another connection, viz: Cain was the first murderer, and therefore stood first. Jesus was crucified between two thieves, and a murderer let loose in his place. Luke 23 : 18, 19. This placed the murderer in Jesus' place. We now come up to the time when God left the Union in Clay, which represented Jesus leaving earth. Pierce and Buchanan are the two thieves, and Abraham the murderer, now last, and in Jesus' place, first last ; just as Jesus said, there are first which shall be last, and last which shall be first. Thus these connections come in just as though the master builder had laid the plan.

Again : God drove the man out of the garden, and placed at the east end a flaming sword to keep the way of the Tree of Life. Gen. 3 : 24. You will see here that he did not drive the woman out of the garden. Also, that he says man, he drove the man out, showing most conclusively that it is a type. Had he said he drove Adam out, then it would have been represented here by driving the Democrats out. But as it is it means drive the power out that is destroying the Garden of the Lord. We now have the sword at the east of the garden, turning every way to keep the way of the Tree of Life. I stated in the Bridegroom that Eve was the germ of the Tree of Life. God also was in the midst of the garden at the time. Jesus comes the seed of the woman, and made of a woman, and God in Him will be the Tree of Life, whose way these swords are keeping. They are guarding the road by which he is to pass to the throne. I have now got through with these connections, and shall come up to Abraham of Old.

The Trinity being established in Abraham, Isaac and Jacob, places this throne in the spirit of Isaac, in whom God stood, hence he left this throne in Clay, who stood as son, Webster as father, and Calhoun as ghost. To prove this, the ghost of Washington appeared to Calhoun a short time before his death. Abraham of old was called to replace the first Adam. The present Abraham was called by the same God to replace the Democrat party, the first Adam. Abraham also represents Esau, who was live ghost for the devil. Abraham is a descendant of Esau. Esau was the head of the Gentile nations. This places Abraham the representative of two persons, of the Democrats, Adam, and of the Republicans, Esau the head of the Gentile nations. Davis represents Isaac and Jacob. Jacob was live ghost for God's Kingdom, and as the ghost is the soul supplied by Eve, it stands in the women, whom Davis is representing. He also represents Isaac, who was the first white child ever born, and a type of Jesus, in whom God will stand as he stood in

Isaac. This places Davis in the shadow of Jesus, implying that the substance is close by. This places the South in the spirit of the Jews, and the North in the spirit of the Gentiles.

Again, the South secede, which represents the Jews leaving Egypt for the land of Canaan. This brings spiritual Egypt and spiritual Canaan into the Union. The North, standing as Egypt, as the South as Canaan. The South has been in bondage from the time the line of thirty-six thirty was stretched across the Union, when the North said, "Thus far thou shalt come, and no farther, but we will go as far over on your side as we please." The Jews were in bondage four hundred years. The South was in bondage forty years; from 1820 to 1860. Again, the Jews made war on the Canaanites, the black men, but could not drive them out, but made them subservient unto them; Judges, 1st chap. The Angel met them afterward and told them that as they had not driven them out that God would not do as He had promised, and that they should not drive them out, and they should be as thorns in their sides—Judges, 2nd ch. 1st to 3d verse. Now, the Gentiles take the place of the Jews, and they make war to drive them out of spiritual Canaan, but mark, they will be as thorns in their sides; this will be as true as that there is a God. When Jesus comes the representative of the stone Joshua sat up, he will be spiritual Joshua, when he will make them subservient unto him, then they will be as thorns in the sides of those trying to free them. My ways are not your ways, neither are my thoughts your thoughts, saith the Lord. We will now pass on to Nebuchadnezzar, the golden head.

Here you must keep in mind that he stood the representative of the first Adam; Eve in Adam, and this Union stood the same. God left it in Clay, when Pierce stood in the place of the golden head. Pierce took the place of General Taylor, in whose term Clay died in the Senate Chamber, the throne of God. Pierce represented Nebuchadnezzar the beast, who represented Cain. Buchanan represented the dead ghost in the devil, Abel. Abel being dead in the devil, was the reason why Buchanan had to fill Pierce's place. It was also the reason why Buchanan could have no wife. The spirit of the woman was dead in the devil, hence he could have no wife. For this purpose God had him raised up in the counsels of the Nation, without a wife, in order to fill the Presidential chair, as the last President of the Union. Abraham comes in the representative of Belshazzar. Abraham stands as Esau who was live ghost of the devil. Had the devil had no live ghost, Nebuchadnezzar could have had no son. Hence, Belshazzar was live ghost for his father, who was in the spirit of Cain, and Abraham being live ghost for Cain, represents Belshazzar. And Davis stands in the shadow of King Cyrus, unto whom all the kingdoms of the earth was given, who will be represented by Jesus, who will receive all the kingdoms of the earth. This connection comes in in carrying out the whole subject, when it will be made more plain.

We now come up to the Pope. The Pope is represented in the Trinity in three kingdoms, as shown above, viz: Rome, Spain and France, as anti-God. The three men who have occupied the Presidential chair since God left in Clay, represent this Trinity as anti-God. In God's place as is the Pope. Pierce represented Rome in spirit, was the type in Nebuchadnezzar, the beast, whose anti-type was Cain. Buchanan represents the spirit of Spain, which was dead ghost in the Pope; her only type was the ghost dead in Cain. Abraham represents the spirit of France, which was, and is, live ghost for the Pope, whose type was Belshazzar, live ghost for his father. Belshazzar's anti-type was Esau, who was live ghost for the devil, and thus these connections all come in complete. Davis is the representative of the live ghost in the women of the South, the spirit of the golden head, whose anti-type was Eve, now represented by her Most Gracious Majesty, Queen Victoria, now occupying the fourth throne in the kingdom, in the image which was the spiritual wife of the dragon, and therefore her Majesty will be the spiritual wife of Jesus, whose throne is in spirit in the women of the South, whom Davis is representing, and thus the whole sums up complete.

Again, shows Abraham beyond a doubt, in the spirit of the dragon. France stands in the spirit of the dragon, and Louis Napoleon has to make the seventh head for him. In the next chapter, which will be on the Revelation, I will prove to you that Abraham and his Cabinet stand in the spirit of the great red dragon, seen in Heaven, with seven heads and ten horns—Rev. 12th ch. This dragon in Heaven was a type, and must be represented three times on earth, in the kingdom of Heaven. This was represented in England, when our fathers rebelled, and is now again represented on this throne, when the South rebelled, and will be again represented in England in Louis Napoleon, when he conquers England to get that spirit to make the seventh head with.

Again, the Revelator says he drew one third part of the stars from Heaven with his long tail. In the Bridegroom I proved to you that the new earth upon which the Revelator saw the new Jerusalem descend was this Continent, and that the flag of the Union was the new Heaven referred to by the Revelator. The stars are set in a blue field to represent the starry throne of God on High. This flag, you must recollect, had just thirty-three stars on it when Abraham was elected, and he had hardly taken his seat before eleven of them were swept off. Eleven is just one third of thirty-three, which proves most conclusively that the flag was the Heaven referred to, and that Abraham and his Cabinet are in the spirit of that red dragon. All these things will be more abundantly proven in other chapters.

I will now notice Abraham, as Belshazzar. Belshazzar made a great feast and drank wine out of the gold and silver vessels of the Lord, and praised the gods of gold and of silver, of brass, of iron, of wood and of stone. At the time this feast was going on the fingers of a man's hand came forth, and wrote over against the candlestick on the plaster of the wall of the King's palace, and the king saw the part of the hand that wrote. This made the joints of his loins loose, and his knees smote one against another—Daniel 5th ch. Just such a feast as this took place in Washington at the time of Abraham's inauguration, notwithstanding the forebodings of the destruction of hundreds of thousands of lives.

Again. The hand-writing on the wall of Belshazzar's palace, was the type of the wall of this Union in the written instrument called the Constitution. Now, as Abraham represents Belshazzar in the connections, so he is "weighed in the balance and found wanting," and his kingdom will be taken from him and given to the Medes and Persians, as will be explained before I close. Moreover, as Belshazzar was slain in that very night, Abraham must make the letter to that type, his reign being the night of the Union. Daniel the first read the hand-writing, and knew the meaning of it. Daniel the second also knows the meaning of it.

Again. Belshazzar and his kingdom worshipped a whole batch of gods who could neither see, hear, nor walk. These are the very kind of gods that Abraham's people are worshipping. I have no doubt they will say that Catholics worship these gods. Well, I will agree to this, that Catholics do worship these gods, and that the Protestants worship the golden god, who is equally as blind, deaf and maimed as the other gods. Nebuchadnezzar made the golden god and set him up on the plains of Dura, while he was yet the golden head. All nations fell down and worshipped this golden god. None but the Hebrew children refused to worship him. For this three of them were cast into the fiery furnace, heated with seven extra heats.

Again. This golden god, made and worshipped whilst Nebuchadnezzar was yet the golden head, belongs to this Union, the golden head in Adam; and if ever a golden god was worshipped faithfully, the people of this Union have done it, they will carry off the palm. But mark now, Abraham, who represents Belshazzar, and also France, has brought the other gods in, and you have now got the whole batch; none of them can see, hear, or walk; they are all dummies. The only God in the world that can see, hear, and walk, is the one that the four Hebrew children worshipped, viz: the God of Abraham, Isaac and Jacob, of old —the same that the Hebrews have worshipped in the golden head, Eve in Adam, and the same they worship now, which is fully proven in the Bridegroom.

Again. I stated above that in the next chapter I would notice old Bonaparte's doings in Moscow. I will also notice them here, as they will come in here as well as there. Mark, old Napoleon helped to cut down the tree that was the type of the extent of this worship, which extended to the ends of the earth. This was a manifestation of the destruction of image-worship with the destruction of the tree and the image, and as he lived in the latter time of their kingdom, the worship could not have long to run after him. Old Napoleon was the cause of Moscow being burnt; this was the type set on earth, of the destruction of great Babylon, as in Rev., 18th chapter. The destruction of that city the type of Babylon in kingdoms, and in the tree, in churches. You must here keep in mind that it is the kingdoms and the worships of the people of those kingdoms, that constitute great Babylon. Popery is the mother of harlots. This makes Protestants her daughters, and as the Union is the toes of the image, of course it belongs to the image, and as Protestantism is the worship in the toes of the image, having come out of England, the feet of the image, both worships belong to the image, one as the mother, the other as her daughter. So when the image is broken to pieces, all the worships will be broken to pieces.

Again. The destruction of old Bonaparte's army of four hundred thousand men on his retreat from Moscow, set the type on earth of the supper of the great God, as in Rev. 19: 17 to 21, inclusive, which read, in part, as follows: "And I saw an angel stand in the sun, and he cried with a loud voice, saying, to all the fowls that fly in the heavens, come and gather yourselves together unto the supper of the great God. That ye may eat the flesh of kings, and the flesh of captains, and the flesh of mighty men, and the flesh of horses, and of them that sit on them, and the flesh of all men, both free and bond, both small and great. And I saw the beast, and the kings of the earth, and their armies, gathered together to make war against him that sat on the horse, and against his army." This great supper will be summed up in fighting the great battle of Armageddon, as in Rev., 16th chapter. This type was set on earth by the destruction of old Bonaparte's army, and this war in the Union commences this supper, standing where it ought not, as Jesus said. The personage riding the horse will be Jesus.

Again. About the time of the burning of Moscow, and of the destruction of this army, a theatre was burned in Richmond, Virginia, the capital of the State. In this conflagration many lives were lost. This set the type on this continent, the New World. Now, when Abraham comes to the throne, in the spirit of Belshazzar and Napoleon, the first and last heads of the dragon, the letter is being made to the type by the destruction of the Union, a nation. And whilst I am writing this chapter, the news arrives of a great calamity in Santiago, the capital of Chile, where two thousand women lost their lives by the burning of a church. The theater has got into the Church. Mark, now, this is the head of all churches on earth, and all the kingdoms and Churches on earth constituted great Babylon. All the known world constitute great Babylon, Protestants included.

Again. No one can read the account of that calamity, but must see with a moment's reflection, that it was the spirit of the beast that brought it about. A priest, direct from the Pope, who is the beast, the eighth but of the seven, had just arrived in Santiago. He informed the officiating priest that his illuminations were nothing compared to those in Rome, when the officiating priest told him that he would give him one such as the world had never seen before. He was faithful to his word, and the result you all know. Now could it have been possible for this priest to not have come there, does any one suppose the calamity would have taken place? I think not. But God's time having arrived, that spirit granted the devil had to do its work. You ask, why could it not have been done in the Union, or in the Old World? Answer, the fire nationally had commenced in the Southern States, where it ought not, so this must take place in a southern country, standing where it ought not.

Again : This fire is the forerunner of the seven extra heats of Nebuchadnezzar's furnace, which was the type of the seven vials of God's wrath which he is coming to pour out on the earth, for the purpose of destroying the mother of harlots and her daughters, who have been worshipping gods who can neither see, hear, nor walk. All worships in the world stand in the image, and golden god, and are all harlot worships. All the churches have now got the theatre in them, all fitted up to suit the golden god. Not one in ten but what goes there to see and be seen. Just what people go to the theatre for. Then come out of her, my people, that ye be not participators of her sins, and that ye receive not of her plagues. Therefore shall there come in one day death and mourning and famine, and she shall be utterly burned with fire, for strong is the Lord God who judgeth her, thus saith the Lord. Rev. 18: 4th and 8th. Yes, all the churches, except the Jewish and Friend Quakers, stand in the spirit of the beast—in the spirit of the devil. They are the blind leading the blind, and will all fall in the ditch together. Then come out of her, come out of her quickly, as not a church edifice will be left standing by the year '71. I do not mean to say they will be burned with fire, but I mean to say that not one stone will be left on another. Let this suffice on this head.

Now, a few words more with Abraham as Belshazzar. I stated above that the Constitution of the Union was set in type by the handwriting on the wall of Belshazzar's palace. In the Bridegroom I proved to you that the wall had fallen down, and that the city had no gates any more. This was proven by Abraham sending Vallandingham out South. The same God that called Abraham makes him act, and therefore made him do this as proof of no gates. I will now add another evidence not given in them. In Abraham's answer to the Democratic Committee of New York, his quotations are entirely from the original Constitution, not taking one word from the Articles. This places the Union back to the first Congress when it had no gates; these Articles being passed then and adopted then, and adopted by the States afterward. Positive proof that there are no gates to the city, and positive proof that Jesus is coming as the letter to the type of Randolph as President. I now repeat, as in the Bridegroom, that no other man can get into the city as President, there being no gates for him to pass through, and for the same reason Abraham can never get out of the city, and therefore is the only available man if another election is to be held. Moreover, if any other man is elected, Abraham will keep the chair in spite of all opposition, as there are no gates for any one to pass through.

I now pass to notice the Fiery Furnace and Lion's Den. I shall notice these in connection. The three Hebrews cast in the furnace were typical of the Trinity of God. The fourth person seen there was typical of the Body of Jesus in whom the Trinity comes. Read the account. I cannot transcribe it. Daniel, 3d chapter. This fourth personage did not come out of the furnace. This same spirit protected Daniel in the lion's den by closing the lion's mouth. After Daniel was taken out his accusers were cast in, and the lions broke their bones before ever they came to the ground. These things keep in mind.

We now pass on to the Throne seen by the Revelator in Heaven, around which were burning seven lamps of fire, said to be the seven Spirits of God. This was the transferring of the seven extra heats of the furnace to Heaven in the spirit. God having protected those in the furnace by his seven spirits. Rev., 4th chap. In the 5th chapter, 6th verse, we find Jesus taking his Father's throne, as the lion of the tribe of Judah. This transfers the spirit of the lion's den to Heaven. Now, as shown in the Bridegroom, this throne in Heaven, and all connected with it, had descended to earth in this Union, save Him that sat on the throne and the spirit of the seven lamps of fire, which were sealed up in the seven vials of God's wrath.

Again: We now point out the Furnace and Den. South Carolina is the lion's den. We know this by a certain type and letter. The king rolled a stone to the den's mouth, and sealed it with his signet and the signet of his lords. Dan. 6 : 17. A number of ships loaded with stone were sunk at the entrance of Charleston harbor, and sealed with the signet of Abraham and his lords. This proves positively that the entrance to Charleston is the mouth of the den. This makes South Carolina the lion's den. Georgia, Alabama, and Mississippi, constitute the fiery furnace, the four States having constituted the germ of the Confederacy. Hence there is a State for each of the four Hebrew children taken down to Nebuchadnezzar, the spirit of which has passed on down through the beast, and trampled under foot by him down through the image, and now coming out of the toes of the image in a Confederacy, and now the beast is trampling that under foot also.

This is the very reason, and only reason too, why Abraham has not got possession of Charleston ere this. You will see by reading the account that Daniel was the only one who entered by the mouth of the den. His persecutors were cast in, implying that they were cast in over the wall of the den. But as all things in South Carolina, as well as in the other three States, stand in the shadow of Jesus the lion of the tribe of Judah, and the seven spirits of God, Abraham will likely get in both the den and furnace. Indeed, I have several types that show they must get into the den, if not the furnace. But woe to them if Jesus in the Trinity and the seven spirits of God take the furnace and den. Mark, the fire came out of the furnace and slew the men who cast in the Hebrews. By the time that Jesus comes the furnace will be ready for the seven spirits of God, sealed up in the seven vials of his wrath. This will be the fire which will destroy the world of mankind, not the earth, the type of which was set in the burning of Moscow, the Theatre in Richmond, and next in the South in burning cotton and cities, and lastly, in the church at Santiago, Chile. And also set in this city by Abraham in having four hundred thousand stamped envelops, each with a head on it, burned in a furnace in this city, in the first year of his reign. All these things have not been chance-work, but are being done by the spirit granted the devil, consequently done by the fore-knowledge of God, all to carry out his plan, and men machines in his hands.

Again. This is the same Confederacy seen by the Prophet Isaiah, in the 8th chapter, 11th and 12th verses: "For the Lord spake thus to me with a strong hand, and instructed me that I should not walk in the way of these people, saying, Say ye not, A Confederacy, to all them to whom this people shall say, a Confederacy, neither fear ye their fear, nor be afraid." You will see by reading this chapter, that there was a class of people who said "not a Confederacy." The Prophet was sent out and instructed to say not as they did, "not a Confederacy," but a Confederacy to all them who want a Confederacy; and he was told to not fear their fear, nor be afraid. Thus you will see that this Southern Confederacy is a Bible Confederacy. A couple of verses preceding these, read as follows: "Associate yourselves, O ye people, and ye shall be broken in pieces; and give ear all ye of far countries, gird yourselves, and ye shall be broken in pieces. Take counsel together, and it shall come to nought; speak the word and it shall not stand, for God is with us." You will see by this that all the world, or far countries are to be broken to pieces, and this Confederacy has to do it, but not till God is with us.

Again. The 17th and 18th verses. "And I will wait upon the Lord, that hideth his face from the house of Jacob, and I will look for him. Behold, I and the children whom the Lord hath given me, are for signs and wonders in Israel from the Lord of hosts, which dwelleth in Mount Zion." You will see here that Jacob and his children shall be for signs and wonders in Israel from the Lord of hosts, soon after this Confederacy. When you have read this chapter, you will see that they are signs of the coming of Jacob in Jesus, and you will wonder that such is the fact, and that your wise men have not seen it before. Jacob's children have all been represented in a district in the land of Canaan. Again represented in Pagan Rome, and again in Papal Rome, in the image, and still again in the colonies, the toes of the image. And once more represented by the thirteen Apostles. Most certainly, this must be wonderful to you. Mark, all this takes place just after the Confederacy, as in the chapter.

Again. In the very verse succeeding these, the wizards having familiar spirits are mentioned, and the people urged to seek their God, rather than wizards. Your humble servant has been trying for several years to get this doctrine before the people, but for the want of means he has not succeeded. In the meantime three wizards have been here—Jacobs, Anderson, and the prince of wizards—and thousands of people pay their dollars to go and see the wizards, instead of seeking their God, in the way of aiding to publish his doctrine. And thus all these things come in precisely as the plan has been laid. In the very next chapter and 6th verse, is the coming of God, in the following words: "For unto us a child is born, unto us a son is given, and the government shall be upon his shoulder, and his name shall be called, Wonderful, Counsellor, The mighty God, The everlasting Father, The Prince of Peace." This is the very God who is coming to take the Confederacy, when all will be broken to pieces. He says in the verse preceding this, that every battle of the warrior is with confused noise, and garments rolled in blood, but this shall be with burning and fuel of fire. This implies what I have already stated, viz: The destruction of almost every city on earth by fire, in connection with battles. I will here close on this prophecy, as if I get the whole work published, this prophecy, with others, will be fully explained.

Now, as Jesus was born whilst the spirit stood in Judah in Pagan Rome, the devil, and thus the New Testament came out of the Jewish Scriptures, I will connect Peter with this image. This doctrine proves that Jacob descended from God in Isaac, he stood in the place of the first Adam, whom God made with hand. Abraham, Isaac and Jacob, represent the spirit of God in three, one in three; hence God in Jesus, will represent those three. This Jacob was regenerated by God in the Angel Gabriel, God standing in the angel, as he had stood in Isaac, when Jacob was begotten. This angel overshadowed the Virgin Mary just like Isaac had overshadowed Rebecca and begat Jacob. In this way God begat Jesus, his only begotten son. God, mark, is a spirit, and the Angel Gabriel was in an immortal body composed of the Holy Ghost, which is the spirit of God, and in this way Jesus got an immortal body, and was God's first begotten son. Isaac's body being mortal, made Jacob God's first born son, and not first begotten son. This makes the immaculate conception of Jesus much plainer. If there was any immaculacy about it, then there has been more or less about the conception of all children. The Angels Gabriel and Michael will be fully explained in the chapter on the Revelation.

Paul calls this Jesus the Second Adam, the Lord from heaven, implying that he had been the first Adam. So when first Adam, he had a son born unto him, whom the Lord cursed, and thus made him devil. In the spirit of the devil, were all Jacob's children in Pagan Rome when Jesus was born, and crucified. This Jesus chooses twelve Apostles, of whom one turns traitor, and one was elected in his place, which makes thirteen, the same number of his children when Jacob. One of these must represent Reuben, Jacob's first-born son, who defiled his father's bed, in lying with his father's concubine, Bilhah, Rachel's maid. Here keep in mind that Rachel was a type of the spiritual kingdom, and her maid partook of the spirit. Gen. 35: 22. Peter appears to have been chosen for this purpose, as he had Peter prefixed to his original name; he also was the first Apostle chosen. Matt. 10: 2. This, then, settles the matter that he was chosen to represent Reuben. Peter also denied his Master thrice, which represents the Trinity.

We will now notice some conversation between Jesus and Peter. Matt. 15th to 19th. "Jesus said unto his Apostles, But whom say ye that I am? And Simon Peter answered and said, Thou art the Christ, the Son of the living God. And Jesus answered and said unto him, Blessed art thou, Simon Bar-jonah, for flesh and blood hath not revealed it unto thee, but my Father which is in heaven. And I say also unto thee, that thou art Peter, and upon this rock I will build my Church, and the gates of hell shall not prevail against it. And I will give unto thee the keys of the kingdom of heaven, and whatsoever thou shalt bind on earth shall be bound in heaven, and whatsoever thou shalt loose on earth shall be loosed in heaven." You will see in the reading of this closely, that Jesus was to build his Church upon his Father, who was not flesh and blood, and who had revealed to Peter that Jesus was the Christ, the Son of the living God. By reading it and leaving out the words, " And I say unto thee, that thou art Peter," you will see that these words were put there as a peculiar type, all of which will be fully explained before I close.

History informs us that Peter and Paul were crucified in Rome, and that Peter was crucified head down, which implies that the feet died first. That is just the way the image goes out of existence. Now, here keep in mind that the image had its origin with Nebuchadnezzar, the golden head, who stood in the place of the first Adam, as Lord of creation, or all the then known world. And when Nebuchadnezzar became a beast he stood in the spirit of Cain, Adam's first born son. Pagan Rome in this spirit, when Peter was crucified, and of course crucified Peter in conformity with the breaking to pieces the image. So, at the time the spirit was transferred from Pagan to Papal Rome, the spirit of Peter stands in the Pope, in the beast who is the eighth, but of the seven. And thus Peter and Reuben stand together in Popery. Father in son. Mark now, it was the same personage that begat both of these men. Jacob begat Reuben natural, and when Jesus begat Peter spiritual, by a call as an Apostle.

We now pass on up to the feet of the image after king James the First came to the throne in the feet. Then there was a class of people in Holland called Puritans. They were natives of England, but had left England because they thought themselves too pure to live there, hence they had emigrated to Holland. They obtained a Charter from King James, and then emigrated to the new world and settled Massachusetts. Some time after this they banished Anne Hutchison and Roger Williams from their Colony, and soon after hung many witches, (Spiritualists may be thankful they did not live in that age of purity,) and also Quakers. This proves the same spirit which these people condemned in England, followed them to the new world. And it will also be an easy matter to convince anybody that this spirit was the spirit of the devil, as none but devils would hang Quakers, or banish women. And to prove to you that this was the spirit of Peter and Reuben. God made them land on the rock of Plymouth, the rock of Peter, and made them settle the first Colony in the new world, which was settled in the spirit of Reuben, Jacob's first son. Now, these are facts that cannot be got round. I will now show you how that was brought about.

History informs us that these people emigrated to Holland before the union of Scotland with England by a marriage. This union by marriage brought the clay in the feet of the image, as shown above. The Puritans having left England before this took place, took no spirit with them, but of the metal in the image, which was the spirit of the devil. You can here see how the spirit of the devil operates upon mankind. It makes them believe they are more pure than any others, hence, whenever you see men or women professing to be more pure than any others, set it down for a truth that the devil is bigger in than out. This God has given to you for a sign. This also comports with the teachings of Jesus.

Before I proceed further I will notice another item, as evidence of the clay in the feet of the image, viz: England had discovered the east coast of the new world, in 1496, more than one hundred years before king James came to the throne. Two small Colonies had attempted to settle on it, but both were lost. Now, why was this so? Because, God was overruling all things, the time which elapsed between the falling to pieces of Pagan Rome, and the establishing of Papal Rome, had to be represented in the discovery and settling the new world, hence no settlements could be made to remain, until the clay was in the feet of the image, and it had to be made more than a hundred years before. God's plan having been laid thousands of years ago, so as to close out old things by the year 66, or at least commence it on the old world, hence everything had to be done like clock work.

We now come up to the establishment of the Union, under the Constitution, when Peter takes his place as an apostle of Jesus, in Washington. Washington, being the first President, stands in the spirit of Peter, the first apostle. Washington was born and buried in Virginia. Now mark, this leaves Peter the devil in Massachusetts. Now, Peter is placed in a position to use the key to bind on earth and in Heaven, and to loose on earth and in Heaven. This Union, being the kingdom of Heaven on earth, both are together, and the spirit of Peter as an apostle of Jesus, is to have the rule of the kingdom during the time the eleven apostles are being represented in the Presidency, and whoever he binds on earth will be bound in Heaven, and who loosed on earth will be loosed in Heaven. This is the meaning of the keys.

Again, the spirit of Peter, the apostle, leaves Heaven in the death of Henry Clay. This represents Jesus leaving earth. Pierce comes in the representative of Judas, and Buchanan the representative of Matthias. This ends the reign of the apostles of Jesus, when Abraham takes the place of Buchanan, the representative of Peter, the beast. Mark, Abraham stands in the spirit of Belshazzar, and in the spirit of Louis Napoleon. Peter also stands in the Trinity, as beast in Pierce, Buchanan and Abraham.

Again, after the ascension of Jesus, the disciples chose seven men to break bread to the Grecian widows. These seven men were the types of the seven churches of Asia, which the Revelator says were the seven golden candlesticks, which are now represented in the Southern Confederacy, and Davis holding the seven stars in his right hand, in the shadow of Jesus. When Jesus takes his place in the seven spirits of God, which was the type of the seven men chosen, then Jesus will break bread to the Grecian widows. Here you must keep in mind that Jacob, in the devil, in Pagan Rome, conquered Esau in the Greeks, Jesus being born when Pagan Rome stood in Judah, received the spirit of Esau by conquest. The spirit of Pagan Rome being transferred to Papal Rome, stands now where it ought not, in Abraham as Esau, in Rome by conquest. Hence, Abraham has the Greek fire. So, when Jesus comes he must have the birth-right of Esau, which he bought for a mess of pottage, when Jacob. This birth-right will be the sceptre of the old Union, which will bring about thousands of Grecian widows.

I must notice one thing more before I proceed farther, viz: The clay came into the feet of the image in England receiving God's kingdom, and God leaves this Union in a man by the name of Clay. I suppose you think this has been chance work. Well, have it so, then. Now if England received God thus, then it follows as a matter of course that the devil was in possession of England before receiving the clay. Then it also follows as a matter of course, that when God left the Union in Clay, the devil took his place in Pierce, Buchanan and Abraham, representing the Trinity. Now we will prove further that this is the spirit of Peter's rock.

In Deut., 32d chapter, 4th verse, we have the following: He is the Rock, his work is perfect, for all his ways are judgments; a God of truth and without iniquity, just and right is he. You will see here that Moses was speaking of the God of Abraham, Isaac, and Jacob, as the just and righteous God. 15th verse.—But Jeshurun waxed fat, and kicked; thou art waxen fat; thou art grown thick; thou art covered with fatness; then he forsook God which made, and lightly esteemed the Rock of his salvation. Of the Rock that begat thee thou art unmindful, and hast forgotten God that formed thee.—18th verse. In these passages you will see that a certain person is spoken of as having grown fat and forgotten God. And in the 31st verse, as follows: For their Rock is not our Rock, and our enemies themselves been judges. Here you see that two rocks are referred to. These two rocks were the types of God as the Rock of our salvation, and Peter the rock of our damnation, or condemnation. This is made more plain by reading the 30th verse. How should one chase a thousand, and two put ten thousand to flight, except their Rock had sold them, and the Lord had shut them in. You will see by reading the whole chapter that it was prophecyed in Moses, who stood as God, second person in the Trinity, and refers to the very times in which we now are. When God comes, one will chase a thousand and two put ten thousand to flight, because their Rock is not our Rock.

Again: God is a rock, and Jesus is the little stone cut out of the mountain without hand, which is to break the image to pieces, as in Daniel, 2: 34th and 45th. Peter the Rock landed on the rock of Plymouth. The rock of Plymouth was a type of God; and Peter landing on it shows he was anti-God—in God's place—precisely as the type set by Jesus. Also, Jesus was the Stone out of the Mountain; and it was him that set this type with Peter. Hence Peter stands as the rock Moses referred to when he said their Rock is not our Rock. This Rock now stands in Abraham, who stands in God's place, as did Peter on the rock of Plymouth, and as does Peter in the Pope who has grown fat and kicked, and Peter in Abraham has kicked when he ought not.

Now, under the reign of Peter the Beast the feet of the image are completed in Peter's Rock. Mark, Peter in Popery places the image in the spirit of Peter the Rock. Hence we now have the golden feet, the silver feet, the brass or copper feet, and the iron feet, as an iron mountain has recently been discovered in Washington Territory. Hence the feet of the image are now completed in the golden gods, silver gods, copper or brass gods, and iron gods, and now ready to be broken to pieces. You must now keep in mind that him who has more than two feet runs his race the sooner; the image goes out feet foremost; and as the finishing of the toes is the finishing of the feet so the mashing or breaking the feet to pieces first is breaking the toes; and as breaking the image to pieces will be accomplished only by the destruction of life, woe to the feet business. I don't name these things because I find fault with anything being done. I name them to show you that you are machines in God's hand, and must fulfill his plan.

I will now close Peter by a brief revisal. Peter standing the same to Jesus as Cain to the first Adam, and Jesus being born when the spirit was in Judah in Pagan Rome, places Peter in the place of Jacob at the head of Papal Rome. The spirit of Peter the spiritual adviser of the Pope, whilst the spirit of Reuben is lawgiver in the Pope, and thus the Pope stands as anti-god. Again, these two spirits pass the ocean in the

Puritans, and land on the rock of Plymouth. The rock of Plymouth being typical of God, and those spirits landing on it, implies they are anti-god, and remain in Massachusetts as anti-god for the time being. Peter as an Apostle takes his place in Washington, whence the spirit remains until the death of Clay, when God leaves the Union, which represents Jesus leaving earth. When Jesus left earth he had eleven Apostles. God left the Union in Taylor's Presidential term, who was the eleventh President. Pierce comes in as Judas; Buchanan as Matthias. Here mark, Matthias was elected before the eleven tongues descended upon the Apostles. Buchanan was elected before the telegraph cable was laid. After the descent of the cloven tongues, Peter became leader, and this made the Disciples choose seven men as above. After Buchanan, Abraham comes in as leader in the spirit of Peter. So when he takes the throne the Disciples have set up the seven golden candlesticks, with the seven stars in the right hand of him in the midst, all in the shadow. Now, you must certainly see this as plain as noonday.

Again, a further evidence: Abraham and Louis Napoleon are both in the same spirit, both after conquest, and both standing where they ought not. You must be aware that Napoleon did not start out until Peter in Abraham led the way.

I will now notice Reuben. Reuben laid with his Father's concubine. Gen. 25 : 23. The Pope being in that spirit has no doubt laid with his Father's concubines. He being anti-god he must act the part set in type by Reuben—Jacob's first begotten son; and as God comes in Jesus His first begotten son, he will find the Pope lying with His concubines.

Again: Massachusetts stands in the same spirit, and when you take into consideration the fact that the maids given to Jacob by his wives, for wives, were black women, then you need not be surprised at the course Massachusetts has been pursuing ever since the birth of the Union, in stealing the blacks from the South. Neither need you be surprised at the number of amalgamated marriages in that State.

Again: John Brown loosed the devil for a little season. In the last President's term he came out of Massachusetts and passed into Virginia where Washington the Apostle Peter was buried, and there commenced the devil's work, for which he was hung, and from that time the spirit has been loose. Now, you can see what spirit it was that has produced this great strife. You can also see why it started soon after God left. It commenced in Pierce's reign, in Kansas, and thus continued until the hanging took place, when it was spread broadcast over the land, and must spread from here throughout the whole world. Again, you also see why Abraham had to come into all the radical notions of Massachusetts. Abraham must come into it to get the spirit of Peter and Reuben. He wants the South to lie with him, but he will come out missing this time. You can now see that the spirit of this whole war has come out of Massachusetts.

This will also account for Butler's course in New Orleans, as well as for all other such acts, or similar acts perpetrated throughout the war. In fact, if you will penetrate the veil with this light, you can see how this whole matter has been hid in the woman, as was the woman hid in Adam, and now comes out in a throne out of the old Union standing in the women of the South, whilst Cain is trying to kill Abel, who is the representative of the women. I don't name these things because I find fault with them; no, but to show you that God is ruling, and not man.

The finishing link in Peter: Jesus said to Peter: "Get thee behind me, Satan, thou art an offence unto me, for thou savorest not the thing that be of God, but those that be of men."—Matt. 16, 23. These words stand in connection with Peter the Rock. Jesus ascended up to Heaven and left Peter behind him, when he became leader. Peter stands in Popery as leader—anti-god. Peter the Apostle stood in Washington. God left the kingdom in Clay, and now Peter comes in Abraham as live ghost for Satan, behind God, savoring the things that be of men and not those that be of God, and thus making a complete letter to the type.

A little more light on the binding on earth and in Heaven, and loosing on earth and in Heaven. The Pope stands in Peter, his kingdom is earth. That spirit stands in Abraham in Heaven, as the Union is the kingdom of Heaven. This brings the same spirit in Heaven where it does the same work that it done in Popery, viz—persecute all opposed to it.

Once more. " For the Son of Man shall come in the glory of His Father with His Angels, and then He shall reward every man according to his works. Verily I say unto you, there be some standing here which shall not taste of death till they see the Son of Man coming in His kingdom." 27th and 28th verse of the same chapter. This ends the conversation with Peter as the Rock. You will see that all this was connected in the conversation with Peter, as is typical, and will be fulfilled when the Son of Man comes, which must be before Abraham leaves the Chair of State, when that power vested in him must get behind Jesus, as it is not the power of God, but of the devil or satan. This will be its destruction and the establishing of the Church of Christ upon the Rock of Peter by conquest, as shown above. I will have more to say on this part of the subject in future chapters.

Now, having got through with Peter, I shall go back to Daniel and bring the whole matter up and carry it out to the end, showing the fulfillment of the prophecy of Daniel. After which I will connect some more items not yet noticed in Daniel.

Daniel saw in his night vision, the same in which he saw the four beasts, one like unto the son of man, come in the clouds of Heaven. This person was brought before the ancient of days, and there was a great dominion given him, which should never be destroyed—7, 13th and 14th verses. The same spirit that saw this in Daniel stood in Jesus as the son of man. He, in Matt. 24—30, Mark 13—26, and Luke 21—28 tells the people that he would again come in the clouds of Heaven, or that he would again come, and when he did he would come in the clouds of heaven. In those chapters He gives an account of his coming, saying that great tribulations should be suffered by the people, and that that day should come as a snare upon the whole earth—Luke 21—35. The Revelator, St. John, speaks of this same coming in the clouds of Heaven, just in advance of the seven golden candlesticks, in these words: " Behold, he cometh with clouds, and every eye shall see him, and they also which pierced Him, and all kindreds of the earth shall wail because of Him." This wailing denotes great tribulation. And Him being seen by those who pierced Him, implies that the spirits in the spirit world will also see this manifestation, Rev. 1—7.

Now keep in mind that the thirteen Presidents have been represented, and the throne in God's place in Abraham, and the seven men represented who broke bread for the Grecian widows, which stand in seven States as the golden candlesticks. Also keep in mind that Jesus conferred himself upon Saul of Tarsus, soon after the seven men had been chosen, as in Acts, 9th ch. Consequently the cloud must bring Jesus as the letter to the type of conferring himself upon Saul, whilst Abraham occupies the throne, and whilst these seven States are under the flag on which the seven stars are. You will see by this that there is no possibility of these things passing away before the cloud comes with the Son of Man. One thing is, however, true, viz: As the South now stand in the spirit of the apostles of Jesus, and as they all forsook Him when He was crucified, so the manifestation of this must be made in forsaking Davis. But if they all forsake him it don't destroy the spirit of the throne, as it stands in the women. None followed Jesus but Peter, and he followed Him to the Judgment bar, when he denied Him thrice. So, Peter in Abraham, must follow Davis to the Judgment bar of God, when he will deny him thrice. Again, this must bring Jesus before Abraham leaves the throne. The cloud will descend some place on the Pacific coast, and I think, near this city, when will be such a time as has never been witnessed on earth. From here He will pass to the East by steamship, in the wake of the Japan Embassy, and take the throne of the seven candlesticks. This will represent the personage seen by Daniel in his third vision—Daniel 10th, 5—6. Keep in mind this personage was seen by Daniel, between the two Bonapartes. It stands between the great king understanding dark sentences, 8, 23, and the vile man, 11, 21. The former is also mentioned the second time, as above shown, in 19th verse. So this personage seen by Daniel, must stand on earth in the reign of this vile, Louis Napoleon.

Again : then will be measured out to Abraham the same measure he has has been meting out to Davis, shaken down, heaped up and run over. And he that leadeth into captivity, must be led into captivity, and he that killeth with the sword, must be killed with the sword—Rev. 13: 10 This, you see, will entirely destroy the North. Jesus will get Esau's birthright by conquest, conquer the North, and extend the garden of the Lord over the whole of it. Again : Jesus will take the Southern Confederacy, as the Lion of the Tribe of Judah, in the spirit of Daniel in the Lion's den, and the Hebrew children in the fiery furnace, when the seven spirits of God set in type by the seven extra heats of the furnace, will sweep everything from before it, as did the fire that came out of the furnace and slew the men who cast the children in. Then those of Abraham's forces in the lion's den will be suddenly destroyed, as were the bones of those broken, who were cast into the den, ere they came to the ground. This will settle the business in this Union, by a lasting peace.

Whilst this is going on in the new world, Louis Napoleon will be at his work, and before the close of 66, will have conquered England, and set up the abomination that maketh desolate, as in Daniel, 11, 31, and in 8 : 13. This will drive her Majesty, Queen Victoria, to this union of Jesus, when she will unite her kingdom with his by a marriage. This will represent the second fleeing of woman, in Rev. 12, 14, where she will remain for time, times and half time, which, at the lowest computation, will be three years and a half. She is to flee as with the two wings of a great eagle. These two wings will be represented by the two side wheels of the steamship Great Eastern. This ship was built to represent Noah's Ark, and is the only ship ever built as large as the ark. As Noah's ark saved God's natural man, and brought him down on this side of the flood, from whom descended his natural kingdom, so must this great ship save God's natural kingdom, and bring it down on this side of the Ocean, from whom must descend God's Spiritual kingdom.

Again : This will give the man-child the iron rod to rule the nations with, as in Rev. 12: 5, 12 and 15; also 2: 27. This iron rod will be kingdom of England, the iron kingdom in the image, which will be the iron rod in the hand of Jesus. Then he will go forth and redeem the mother. This will cause two great struggles, as in Rev. 14: 11 and 23. The first will be on the ocean, when Joseph's pit will have water in. In this Louis Napoleon will be defeated, when he will flee from England, setting her on fire first, as the type set by the old Czar, in Moscow. This will verify Daniel, in 7, 11, where he says the fourth beast was destroyed and given to the burning flames. The second struggle will take place outside of England, on the field of Waterloo, where the tree was cut down. This battle will dig the stump of it up and plant in its place the tree of life. Then the little stone will have broken the toes and feet of the image to pieces.

After this Louis Napoleon will retreat to the valley of Jehosaphat, where the great battle of Armageddon will be fought. God calls it the valley of decision. There will be decided the fate of all nations of earth. This battle will be fought between God and the Devil, and will crumble to dust all thrones on earth, and upon their ruins will arise the throne of Almighty God, before whom every knee must bow, and every tongue confess that Christ is Lord, to the glory of God the Father. In this battle Louis Napoleon will have ten powers to help him, which will be the ten horns of the great dragon, as in Rev. 17: 12. They have received no power as kings yet with the beast, only been with him an hour. Hence the time has not yet arrived for these kings to have their power with the beast, neither will it, until after England is conquered. By reading from the twelfth verse to the end of the chapter, you can see the result. This will complete the supper of the great God, as above stated.

Again: this great battle will beat the sword unto the plough-share, and the spear into the pruning-hook, and conquer Rome, Spain and France, and unite them to the kingdom of Jesus; just as Daniel says in regard to the other three beasts. He says their dominion shall be taken away, but their lives spared for a season and a time. This you see then, completely verifies Daniel's vision of the four beasts that represent the image. It also breaks the image to pieces, when there will be no place found for it as kingdoms. It also verifies that of Jesus to Peter, saying: "On this rock I will build my Church, and the gates of Hell shall not prevail against it." Mark, now, Jesus' Church will be the kingdom God sets up in the days of these kings, which he sets up on the rock, Peter by conquest. Then He will start the regeneration, when immortal children will be born, instead of mortal ones, and as the grave is Scripture hell, the gates of hell cannot prevail against it. None of these children will ever be buried. The immortal kingdom, or church, call it which you please, is in the seed of Jesus, which is the seed of God, hence Jesus builds his church on the rock of God, with the rock, Peter, for a conquest. This is the sum and substance of the whole of that matter.

Again: this great crisis about the close of 71, when the Queen's mission of about three and a half, or four and a half years, will be out in the new world where she fled to when the throne will be moved to England, when Jesus will receive his father David's throne, when him and his wife will occupy it jointly, as did Mary and William. Then will be represented the parable of the sheep and goats. You will see at a glance, the beauty of the parable. It says all the nations shall be gathered before Him. Here all nations will be before Him, represented by their kings, when He will separate one nation from another, as a shepherd divideth his sheep from the goats. Those nations that represent the sheep He will place upon His right hand, admit into His kingdom. Those representing the goats place on the left hand, destroy them from off the earth. This will bring the whole world into God's kingdom, when the stone will have become a great mountain, filling the whole earth, as in Daniel, 2: 35. And which also will fulfil Daniel, 7: 14, and 27, when the greatness of the kingdom under the whole Heaven will be given to the people of the saints of the Most High, and all shall serve and obey him.

Again. Then the world will be divided into twenty-four parts, each part represented by a Minister residing at the capital, verifying. the words of Jesus to his Apostles, " Whoever will be greatest among you let him be your Minister. And whoever will be chiefest, let him be your servant. Matt. 20: 26, 27. Jesus said, "I come not to be served, but to serve. Luke 22: 27; John 13: 13, 14. Jesus the King, the servant of the whole world. The Ministers the Apostles, or Elders around the throne in heaven. Mark, heaven will be on earth then, and the Elders represented by the Ministers, who will receive the laws from Jesus on the throne, as Moses received them from God in the cloud. These Ministers will send the dispatches to their different departments. These departments will be governed by Governors, as set in type in England. All difficulty between the people will be settled by arbitration. All Judges, Juries and Courts, will be dispensed with. Such is a rough outline of the summing up of old things, and starting the new things in their places.

I will now notice some items connected with the summing up of matters. 1st. The reader will see that it is impossible for those ten horns of the dragon to have appeared yet. In order to make this more plain, I must cite you to one fact, viz : When the Revelator was in heaven, the Lord made all there seen by him pass before him, when he wrote the same. Afterward, God made men, as tools in his hand, build up all things as passed before the Revelator, commencing with the throne of the little horn. Now, we not having arrived at that point on earth, in which the angel said unto John, " Come here, I will show unto thee the judgment of the great whore that sitteth upon many waters. Rev. 17: 1. You will see that the seven vials of God's wrath had just been poured out, as in the 16th chapter. Hence the angel had called John to see the effect that the pouring out of these vials would have on the great whore. In the 16th chapter is the great battle of Armageddon, and as that cannot be fought until after England is conquered and redeemed, so the ten horns cannot be represented by ten kingdoms, hence the Revelator said they had only been one hour with the beast. This will be literally verified about the year 68, when great preparation will be made to fight the great battle of Armageddon, when they must give their power to the beast until the word of God is fulfilled. 17: 17. This will close up with the year '71.

Again: These ten kingdoms form no part of the seven heads of the dragon, but are to help Louis Napoleon make the seventh head, he being the acting spirit for the Pope, the beast. It being the serpent's head that has got to be made, it will require much more power, than the making of either of the other heads required. These ten kings will be ten separate kingdoms, consequently ten beasts, not one beast with ten horns, but ten beasts with each a horn.

Again. The beast is the eighth, but of the seventh. You will see here that it takes eight heads to make a best with seven heads. Had the beast, who is the eighth, no head, it would be a carcass with seven heads. A beast must have a head ; without a head there could be no such thing as beast, or any other living thing. The beast stands the same in the midst of his seven heads, as anti-god, that Jesus does in the midst of the seven spirits of God, set in type by the seven golden candlesticks, and Jesus in the midst. So, when Jesus comes in the seven spirits of God, he will take the place of the beast in the midst of his seven heads, as anti-God. This will destroy the beast and all that pertains to him.

We will now notice Daniel's beast with ten horns, and the little horn, which, as proven above, is England. You will see that had England not united those ten horns into the little horn, there would still be ten kingdoms there, and consequently ten beasts, with each a horn. Therefore, in order to constitute a beast wi h ten horns, it requires the union of ten beasts into one. This is precisely the way England stands. She stands in the spirit of those ten horns, and is the beast with ten horns. Pagan Rome fell into ten kingdoms to represent ten of Jacob's children in the devil. These were again united in the spirit in Papal Rome, in the feet of the image, in the devil. This being a part of the fruits of God's kingdom, and the other part is the birth of this Union, as a kingdom for Jesus.

We will now apply some of the sayings of this little horn. In Daniel's night vision, he beheld until thrones were cast down, and the Ancient of days did sit. I stated above that these thrones were the States of this Union. Mark, thrones being cast down, implies they did exist. Dan. 7 : 9. In the 11th verse, the little horn spake great words, for which the beast was destroyed, and given to the burning flames. This took place as a type when these thrones were established. The war of independence was the time these words referred to, when the spirit of the beast was on the throne of England in George the Third, when our fathers rebelled.

Again. Now that same spirit is on the throne of the Union, and the South rebelled. The same great words are spoken again, 7 : 24, 25, 26; but this time the judgment shall sit, and his dominion taken, and destroyed unto the end. This will be done by the personage coming in the cloud, as seen in the night vision, which will cast down these thrones, as in 7 : 9. This will destroy the sceptre of the Union, as in the 26th verse. Then England will be given to the burning flames, and the dominion of the other three beasts taken away, as in 11th and 12th verses, one after the other, just as stated above.

Again. In the second vision, Daniel also saw some of the wonderful work of this little horn. Dan. 9. This stands in connection with Daniel overhearing the saints discussing the question of how long it should be until the transgression of desolation, to give both the sanctuary and the host to be trodden under foot, which, as proven above, is the "abomination of desolation" mentioned in 11: 31, which Louis Napoleon, the vile man, must set up in conquering England, and when in his possession will speak the great words, as in 8: 10, 11, 12. Jesus said, "When ye shall see the abomination of desolation standing, where it ought not, let him that readeth understand." This abomination is now standing in this Union, where it ought not, in heaven. Mark 13: 14. This fulfils the very words of Daniel. 8: 10. "And it waxed great, even unto the hosts of heaven, and it cast down some of the hosts of the stars on the ground and stamped on them." Mark now, as proven above, Abraham is in the spirit of Louis Napoleon, and as shown above, he is the devil in heaven, and has with his long tail drew one third part of the stars from heaven, which was eleven. Now, as a star is the emblem of a State, the States are the stars he is stamping upon with the feet of his army. Mark, whatever his army and navy do, are the doings of Abraham. Thus everything goes precisely as Daniel said.

Once more Daniel says that this vile man shall honor the god of forces, and a God, whom his father's knew not, shall he honor, with gold and silver, and with precious stones, and pleasant things. Thus shall he do in the most strongholds with a strange god, whom he shall acknowledge and increase with glory, and he shall cause them to rule over many, and shall divide the land for gain—11: 38, 39. All this Abraham is doing, and will do, standing where it ought not. He is even now dividing the land for gain. Taking the land from the owners and giving it to his own people, those who are with him in setting up the abomination that maketh desolate, out of place. You tell me that in this enlightened age of the world, men, as free agents, could do this. I tell you there is not a word of truth in it. God rules the armies of Heaven, as well as the inhabitants of the earth, and none can stay His hand, or say unto Him, what doest Thou ? They must all acknowledge before this desolation is over, as did Nebuchadnezzar—Daniel, 4: 35. I don't say aught in malice. Abraham is doing just what God is making him, and none can stay his hand, or say unto him, what doest thou ? The Most High God ruleth the kingdoms of men, and giveth it to whomsoever He will, and sitteth the basest of men upon thrones—4, 17. God is continually bringing good out of evil, and very often, to accomplish this, places the basest of men on thrones, as the type set in Joseph, being by his brethren sold into Egypt, out of which came much good.

We will now notice another point in connection with the toes of the image—Daniel, 2: 42, 43. And as the toes of the feet were part of iron, and part of clay, so the kingdom shall be partly strong, and partly broken. And whereas, thou sawest iron mixed with miry clay, they shall mingle themselves with the seed of men, but they shall not cleave one to another, even as iron is not mixed with clay. The kingdom referred to here is the fourth kingdom, England the feet of the image, which is partly strong and partly broken, by the dividing of England into the Union, which are the toes of the image. Had there been a crown worn in the Union it would have made a kingdom of it, but as this has not been the case, it stands as a part of England, only divided, which takes away part of her strength.

Again : the toes of the image should not cleave together, that is, the worship that constitutes the iron and the clay should not cleave together, should not be united in Church and State, as had been the four kingdoms which represent the image. They shall mingle themselves with the seed of men. Now, who are meant here as mingling with the seed of men ? Answer: the seed of the beast, evidently Papal worship, whilst the Protestants stand as the seed of men. These shall not cleave together. in church and state, but shall mingle themselves together, live in the Union, each protected in his rights. Now, when the little stone comes, he will break the image to pieces This will break Papalism and Protestantism to pieces, when they will pass to the four winds or Heaven, and no place found for them. This will sweep away the seed of the beast and the seed of man, making room for the seed of woman, the seed of God, the seed of Jesus, who was made of woman. This will bring about a great nationality, which will be the true worship of God, who will then be judging the world in righteousness by that man whom he hath ordained, Jesus Christ, in whom will be God.

Now I have got through with those points, I shall now sum up and connect the golden head, and some other points, in Daniel. But before I do this I must notice two historical facts, and then some items connected. personally with Queen Victoria. 1st, then, some few weeks since, I was in conversation with a gentleman of this city, on the subject of the doctrine, when he asked me if I knew where the stone was that Jacob set up at the time he had the vision of the ladder—Gen. 18th ch. I told him I did not, as it was not traced down in the Scriptures further than the close of Joshua's life. But in the Bridegroom I had pointed out that Jesus was the representative of that stone, and that he would be the house in whom God would have his abiding place. He then told me that the literal stone was under the chair of state of England. I asked him if it was a matter of history. He told me it was, and could be found in Goldsmith's History of England. This, then, places that stone under the Queen every time she occupies the chair of state. Keep this in mind.

2nd. This gentleman then asked me if I knew where the crown of David was. I told him that I did not know where the literal crown was, but that in the Bridegroom I had proved that England received God's kingdom in the union of Scotland with England, by a marriage, in which the spirit of the crown of Scotland went to England, but did not know that David's crown was in Scotland. He then told me that it was in Scotland. I asked him if it was a matter of history. He said it was, and could be found in the history of the kings of Scotland, and it was the identical crown which David wore. And furthermore, that the crown was one stolen from the king of Egypt, by his daughter, and given to the Hebrews when in Egyptian bondage. Now, these things being matter of history, can you longer doubt the truth of my doctrine? Again, there can be no doubt that this was the first crown ever made on earth, and that as Nimrod was the first great leader of the people, that he had it made. And no doubt that it was set in type for David, or God's kingdom, by the crown made for Aaron.

I shall now notice the items connected with her most gracious Majesty, Queen Victoria. 1st. Some six years ago she received a golden star, a present from a king far in the east. This star is the representative of the star that guided the wise men of the East to the babe of Bethlehem, as in Matt. 2d ch. 2d. Some year or two after this, her majesty received a golden bedstead, as a present from the Rajah of Cashmere, worth seven hundred and fifty thousand dollars, as also a Cashmere tent. The Rajah certainly knew that she would have to camp out, or he would not have sent her a tent. 3d. A year or two after that she also received a golden crown, as a present from a king far in the East. I have forgotten the kingdoms from which these presents came, but that don't destroy their value, neither does it destroy the fact of her having received them. Keep these things in mind now, whilst I go back to the first Adam, and trace up the golden head.

Here keep in mind that Adam was the golden head whilst Eve was in him, and when she was taken out of him she was the golden head, and in the garden of the Lord. Now, for the sake of carrying the illustration more forcibly, we will call God the golden God. He stood beyond Adam, and Eve on this side of Adam. We now come up to the call of Abram. H and Sarah replace Adam and Eve at the head of God's natural kingdom; the golden head on this side of Abraham, and the golden God on the other side. God promises Isaac, and afterward in him as the second person in the Trinity. This brings the golden God on this side of the golden head. Keep these things in mind.

Again : The next thing we find worthy of mention, was a golden calf made by Aaron, Ex. 32d ch. This calf came whole out of the fire, 24th verse. Moses took the calf and burnt it and ground it to powder, and strewed it upon the water and made the people drink it, 20th verse. Nebuchadnezzar next comes in as the golden head of the image, Eve in Adam, when he makes a golden God and sets him up on the plain of Dura. This places the golden God this side the golden head. This golden God was a type of Jesus. Now, when Jesus comes the representative of this golden God, and takes the throne of the germ of the golden head, then her majesty will be between the golden God and Golden calf, the Pope being the golden calf, right where Eve stood between God and the devil.

Again : When the spirit of the Golden Calf in Louis Napoleon conquers the Queen, then she will flee in the Great Eastern, bringing her cabinet and spirit of her throne, together with the golden crown, golden bedstead, and tent, and golden star; then will the star guide the wise men of the east to the throne of the babe of Bethlehem, making a perfect letter to the type set. Then the golden head will put the golden crown upon the head of the golden god, and when the proper time arrives they will lay on the golden bedstead, and the fruits will be golden gods and golden heads. None of your oak trees any more, but golden gods and golden heads.

I will now show you the type set for these golden gods. When Rachel, who was the type of the spiritual kingdom, left her father's house, she stole his gods.—Gen. 31 : 30th and 32d verses. These gods she hid under the camel's furniture, and sat upon them.—34th verse. So when her father entered the tent (you see here is the tent) to search for them she made such a lawful excuse that he never asked her to get up.—35th verse. This was the type set for the birth of Gods. Jesus was born from under Mary, as were these gods placed; and just as true as was he born from under a woman just so true will gods be born from under Queen Victoria as the type set by her sitting on the Chair of State, and that stone under her, which Jacob said should be the house of God. This will start the second birth, and when completed the world of mankind will be immortal. God in all, and death, God's last enemy destroyed, then every heart will be a fit temple for the Holy Ghost to dwell in, and God's house completed. This is the summing up of the golden head. Now, let me ask any sane man or woman what fault they can find with this. Here no doubt one will say the Queen is too old to have children. Remember Sarah of old and then you will not think so—more especially as the same God will be in Jesus that took away Sarah's barrenness; and he can take away all the barrenness the Queen will have.

Again : The Queen is the only heir now living to that throne; and as the two thrones must be united by a marriage, as Jesus being the seed of the woman in man, there is no alternative but the marriage must take place between Jesus and the Queen. According to the law of David's kingdom, the Prince of Wales is not an heir to that throne, and therefore never will occupy it, from the very fact that he is not of the seed of the king. There was no seed on the throne, nothing but the soul, hence the soul comes out of the union in the women of the Southern Confederacy. Jesus comes with the immortal body, and must therefore have the woman, who wears the crown of the soul on a throne.

Again : The four Hebrew children taken to Nebuchadnezzar were of the seed of the king and princess. It is reasonable to suppose that Daniel was of the seed of the king, as he was cast into the lion's den.

Furthermore, we find that Daniel stood as God in man. In Dan., 9th chapter, 28th verse, he tells Nebuchadnezzar that it belongs to God to reveal secrets. He then goes on and reveals to the king the secrets of the image, and closes by saying the Great God hath made known to the king what shall come to pass hereafter.—45th verse. This shows most conclusively that Daniel stood god in man. Again, we have still further evidence of this fact. Nebuchadnezzar dreamed this dream about the image, and when he awoke he had forgotten it. He then called his wise men together, and requested them to tell him the dream and the interpretation of it. This they could not do, and he therefore decreed their death. Now, why was it that he forgot the dream? Answer—God stood in him. Mark, he was then the golden head of the image, and dreamed the dream, and then left him, when of course he forgot it. God then stood in Daniel, and told him the dream, and then interpreted it for him. This made Daniel God in man, when he went on finishing all the items in connection with the setting up of God's kingdom.

Again: When Darius was placed on the throne of Babylon he placed over the whole kingdom one hundred and twenty princes, and over them three presidents, of whom Daniel was first. Now, as this Daniel was preferred above all others, the king thought to place him over the whole realm.—6: 1st, 2d, and 3d verses. You must here keep in mind that this Union stands as Babylon standing where it ought not, and it now has two Presidents, and when Jesus comes the spirit now in Daniel the second will be transferred to Jesus, when Jesus will stand as Daniel the first, and be made President over the two—will stand as first President—when he will take his father's (David's) throne, as in Luke 1 : 32. This throne is the throne of England, and thus the seed of God heir to the throne of England. By this you will see that it is not possible that the Prince of Wales can ever obtain that throne, as he is not the seed of the king. Then there is no earthly way to get around the fact that her Majesty must be the Christ of Our Lord Jesus. And this will give all the kingdoms of the earth to Our Lord and His Christ, as in Rev. 11: 15. Then the crown of David, now in Scotland, the first crown ever made, will be cast at the feet of him who sits on the throne, followed by all the crowns in the world, as in Rev. 4: 10, 11. This will end the reign of terror on earth, and not until then will it be ended.

Another item in this connection. When her Majesty, Queen Victoria, flees to the kingdom of Jesus, she will letter the type set by Jacob in blessing Judah for the last time. Gen. 49: 10. "The sceptre shall not depart from Judah, nor a lawgiver from between his feet, until Shiloh come, and unto him shall the gathering of the people be." In this connection keep in mind that England stands in the spirit of Judah, and that Jacob comes in Jesus; he was also set in type in the Isle of Man, between the two feet of the image, the two of Judah, the iron kingdom in the image. So when this fleeing takes place, the Queen will bring the sceptre and the lawgiver to Jesus, the promised Shiloh; and unto him the gathering of the people shall be. Yes, unto him will be the gathering of all the nations of the earth.

Again. Woman is the soul of man. This could not be if they were not of God, a part of that never-dying spirit called God. Hence Queen Victoria is the soul of David's throne, and Jesus will be the body of that throne. Hence the Soul of God brings the sceptre and lawgiver to God in Jesus, Jesus himself being the body as immortal as the soul. Hence the sceptre and lawgiver will stand in Jesus and his Christ jointly, both occupying the throne, the Godhead standing male and female, from whom will eminate the laws for the government of the world. Now let this suffice on this head, whilst I notice a few more items in connection with Louis Napoleon.

In the 11th chapter, 27th verse, we are told that certain kings shall speak lies at the same table, but it shall not prosper. The only way that kings speak lies at the same table, is by breaking treaties, and this will no doubt be done ere long, as the angel says that this vile man shall prove deceitful, in regard to the alliance between him and England. There may also a Congress meet; if so, it will be a useless affair, as what will there be done will not be lived up to. Again. Edom, Moab, and the chief of the children of Ammon shall escape his hand. 11th chapter, 41st verse. In the Bridegroom, I proved to you that Moab, was Japan, and Ammon China, and this Union Edom, as in Gen. 36 : 1, 8. Esau is Edom, and as above, Abraham is Esau, hence the Union is Esau. I stated in the Bridegroom that the Union had nothing to fear from Napoleon. But you will see here that this account stands connected with Napoleon, after he has conquered England, and therefore he may make some demonstration against the Union before Jesus comes, or before he bursts out against England. But as Napoleon and Abraham are in the same spirit, I think that it is not at all likely.

Again. You will see by reading the 11th chapter, from the 21st verse, that the same vile man conducts one side of the affair to the end, and then plant the tabernacles of his palace between the seas in the glorious holy mountain. Yet he shall come to his end and none shall help him. This personage is Louis Napoleon. The glorious holy mountain here is the kingdom of God, set up on the ruins of all other kingdoms. Mountains are types of kingdoms. Hence it follows that after Louis Napoleon has been the devil for the time appointed by God, he shall come to his end in God's kingdom without help, implying that he shall die a natural death. I now state what I stated six years ago, viz : that there is not powder and ball enough in the world to kill him. Neither is there enough to kill Queen Victoria. When God has persons born for a certain purpose, they are not to be killed, as was the case with Washington, and old Bonaparte, and as will be the case with the two named above. By this time, no doubt, you will think the devil is God's right hand man. Mark, there could have been no Judas without a Jesus, and therefore no devil without a God. Judas prepared the way for the crucifixion of Jesus, and the devil prepares the way for the crucifixion of the world of mankind. God natural. Everything that is, is right.

I will now notice the last chapter in Daniel. The angel tells Daniel that Michael shall stand up at that time, the great prince which standeth for the children of thy people, and there should be a time of trouble, such as never was since there was a nation even to that same time, and at that time thy people shall be delivered, every one that shall be found written in the book. And many of them that sleep in the dust of the earth shall awake, some to everlasting life and some to everlasting contempt. Mark, this Michael was Daniel's prince, as in the 10th chapter, 21st verse. Here you must also keep in mind that none but Gabriel and Michael knew of the Scripture truth in regard to these matters. Gabriel was first spirit and Michael second spirit in the Trinity, one the Father and the other son. Hence, when Jesus comes, he stands as Michael, Daniel's prince, with the spirit of Gabriel in him representing Father in Son. These are the two candlesticks standing before the Lord of the earth, as in Rev. 11: 4. These were the same two golden pipes emptying the oil out of themselves, as in Zech. 4 : 12. They pass the spirit to man on earth, and rule the armies of heaven, as well as the inhabitants of earth, which will bring about the great calamity mentioned here. This calamity is to take place at the time the vile man rules, as in the 11th chapter.

Again: At that time every one of Daniel's people found written in the book shall be delivered. The book referred to here is the Jewish scriptures, and every one who has lived up to the laws given to Moses in the cloud, will escape this calamity, will escape death, and be delivered from the kings, or rulers, under whom they have lived for the last two thousand years, or from the days of Daniel. That is, those who are alive on earth when Michael stands up for his people. It has nothing whatever to do with those who have died, or with the dead of the Gentiles. Those referred to as sleeping in the dust of the earth, embrace those who are ignorant of coming events, the dust of the earth being the body in which the man lives and sleeps, the sleeping being the same as that in the parable of the ten virgins, where they all slept and slumbered till midnight, when the cry of the coming of the bridegroom sounded, which waked them up. Some shall wake to everlasting life, and some to shame and everlasting contempt. That is, some will wake up at the coming of Jesus as the Messiah, and accept him cheerfully, whilst others will not, and therefore will awake to shame and everlasting contempt, feel guilty. The word, everlasting, has no such thing as an endless meaning in this connection.

3d verse. And they that be wise shall shine as the brightness of the firmament, and they that turn many to righteousness, as the stars forever and ever. Keep in mind that old things must then pass away, and new things take their place, when the wise will shine for their good works. Then men won't be afraid to do God's work for fear they will be evil spoken of. The sum and substance of the whole verse is that good works will be rewarded, whilst evil works will be punished, not as it is now, evil rewarded and good punished.

4th verse. But thou, O, Daniel, shut up the words and seal the book, even to the time of the end, many shall run to and fro, and knowledge increase. Here you see that Daniel was instructed to seal up the book until the time of the end. And at the time of the end many should run to and fro, and knowledge should increase. According to this we must certainly be near the end, as there has never been a time since the world began, in which the people have run to and fro, as now. Moreover, knowledge has never increased so rapidly since the world began, as in the last twenty years, which must be very strong evidence that we are near the end referred to.

5th, 6th and 7th verses. Daniel gives an account of seeing one clothed in linen, asking, how long shall it be to the end of these wonders? The answer was, for a time, times and a half, and when he shall have accomplished to scatter the power of the holy people, all these things shall be finished. You must here keep in mind that this inquiry starts with the scattering of the power of the holy people, hence it commences with the conquest of England, as in 11 : 31. When the sanctuary of strength is polluted, and the abomination that maketh desolate set up. From that time it shall be time, times, and an half. The lowest computation of scripture time, times, and an half, will be three years and a half. The same can be extended up to any number and an half. As the seventh king who is to make the seventh head for the dragon, abide a short space, as in Rev. 17 : 13, it is not likely that this time, times, and an half, will embrace more than three or four years and a half, or five years and a half, at most, inasmuch as the great calamity must close with the year 71. This time, times, and an half, is the same the woman fled for in Rev. 12 : 17, and will be the fleeing of Queen Victoria, which settles the matter in regard to the starting point for the time, times, and an half, in Daniel.

Again : this is the same time, times, and the dividing of time mentioned by the Angel, in his explanation to Daniel, in regard to things seen in the night vision—7th ch. 25th verse. When the little horn was to wear out the saints as it was. This will be represented by Louis Napoleon, when in possession of England. It shall then be time, times and the dividing of time, when the kingdom and dominion, and the greatness of the kingdom under the whole Heaven shall be given to the people of the saints of the Most High, when God shall sit and judge the world. This brings all the time, times and a half to one starting point.

8th, 9th and 10th verses. "And I heard, but I understood not, the n said I, O, my Lord, what shall be the end of these things. And he said, Go thy way, Daniel, for the words are closed up and sealed till the time of the end. Many shall be purified and made white, and tried, but the wicked shall do wickedly, and none of the wicked shall understand, but the righteous shall understand." Here you will see that Daniel said, O, my God, what shall be the end of these things ? And He said, Go thy way, Daniel. This implies that God was there in the Angel Gabriel, and told him to go his way. Then it follows that these are the very words of God. When talking on this subject with people, they invariably say the wicked will cease to do wickedly when God comes. I have always answered right to the reverse, that they would try to kill God. Here God settles the matter by saying they shall continue to do wickedly.

11th verse. "And from the time the daily sacrifice shall be taken away and the abomination that maketh desolate set up, there shall be one thousand two hundred and ninety days." Here you see God settles the matter. Mark, he continues to speak to the end. He says it shall be twelve hundred and ninety days from the time the abomination that maketh desolate is set up, to the end. Mark, now, these are literal days with us, and not prophetic days. This is proven by the fact that they start from the same point at which the time, times and half start from, viz : The setting up of the abomination that maketh desolate, as in 11th ch. 31st verse. And furthermore, God gives these days to explain the time, times and an half, given by the man clothed in linen, to Daniel.

12th verse. "Blessed is he that waiteth and cometh to the thousand three hundred and five and thirty days. This you will see is forty-five days longer than the number just mentioned, which will end forty-five days after the great battle of Armageddon is over. Hence he that is not born until that time will be blessed, inasmuch as there will be no more wars or fighting on earth. The sword will then have been beat into the plowshare, and the spear into the pruning hook, and men learn war no more. This will most certainly be a great blessing to the new-comer. Besides, the famine and pestilence will all have gone by, and trials and troubles ceased. Peace and good-will will then reign on earth among men, and God will be their king, judging the world as a king now judges, the only difference will be that God will be a just and righteous king.

This brings me to the last verse of the prophecy. "But go thy way till the end be, for thou shalt rest, and stand in thy lot at the end of the day." Here you will see that Daniel was promised to stand in his lot at the end of the days. The end of the days referred to here, was used in the same sense as the end of the vision. The time when God sets up the kingdom of which Daniel prophecied. Daniel is the only prophet in the book having this promise from God. Daniel is also the only prophet that prophesied directly of God setting up a kingdom in the days of certain kings. And Daniel was the only prophet having been cast into the lions' den. All these things taken together, and many more that I might name, make Daniel a peculiar prophet, and one worthy of such a promise.

Again. Now, would it be reasonable to think that God intended that the same Daniel, in the same body, should fulfill this promise by standing in his lot at the end of the days? I think not. God knew that Daniel was a mortal man. He also knew that the setting up of that kingdom would be many hundred years after the promise, and therefore could not have intended that same Daniel to stand in person in his lot when God would set up the kingdom. It is therefore reasonable to believe that God designed that a man by the name of Daniel should fill the place alluded to, and also that this Daniel should be a Gentile instead of a Jew. This is the most reasonable, inasmuch as Jesus is coming to unite the Jews and Gentiles, absorb them both, and as the first Daniel was a Jew, as well as the first Abraham, so the second Daniel should be a Gentile, as well as the second Abraham.

Again. The only object God could have had in making this promise, must have been to have a Daniel here as there, and God spake in him here as there, and thus God would give warning of his coming to set up the kingdom referred to. It most certainly would be of no use to have a man here unless for some purpose, and some special purpose too. We have many Daniels here now, no doubt, so unless God speaks in the one sent, no one could tell the difference. Hence the only way to find out the right one, is for him to interpret the image correctly, in four kingdoms, as Daniel the first did. Now, if when you have read the interpretation of the image by Daniel the second, and it agrees with the interpretation of Daniel the first, then set it down for granted that Daniel the second is here in his place, as promised to Daniel the first. Then prepare to meet your God, for behold, the Bridegroom cometh, go ye out to meet him. My doctrine is not mine, but his that sent me.

Now, reader, I have got to the end of this prophecy, and have written only what Daniel's God put on my tongue. I have not said aught in malice; I have not spoken so plain because my sympathies are with the South. No, my sympathies are only with the South, because God has put this doctrine on my tongue. Hence how could I do otherwise than speak it out plain. Had the North seceded from the South, and the new Confederacy appeared in the North, then the North would have been God's garden, and my sympathies would have been with the North. But God's ways are not man's ways, neither are his thoughts man's thoughts. I have said from the time Abraham took the Chair of State, that he would do precisely what he has been doing. And I have said from the first, that he was chosen to fill that place by God himself, and God rules the armies of heaven, and give this as the reason that neither party in Virginia could follow up a victory. God Almighty is ruling, and man is the machine in his hand, and are compelled to do as they have been, and will continue to do. I have stated from the first, that the South must be crucified first, as it is the germ of the throne of Jesus, after which the North must be crucified, and then must follow the crucifixion of the whole world. You see that the words given me in the illustration of this prophecy proves all I have said. I shall now proceed to connect with this Abraham's mission as the representative of Abraham of old.

I will now cite you to the 22d chapter of Genesis, where you will find an account of God tempting Abraham to offer up Isaac, his son, as a burnt offering. Abraham rose up early in the morning, and saddled his ass, took his two young men, and Isaac his son, and clave wood for the burnt offering. He went three days' journey, when he came in sight of the place where the offering was wont to be made. He then put the wood upon Isaac, and he bore it to the place of offering, when the ram was offered in the place of Isaac. Such is a brief statement of the case. Now here I want you to keep in mind that there were none living on earth in that day but Indian tribes, save Isaac, the promised child. It therefore follows that Abraham was an Indian, as had been the first Adam, the red man.

We now come up to the close of the term of the thirteenth President in the New Jerusalem natural. A Convention is called to nominate a President to fill the place of the thirteenth. This Convention meets in a most northwestern city, when God calls a man to represent Abraham of old. This man's name is Abraham, and in order to prove that he was chosen by God to represent Abraham of old, God makes them call the house in which he was nominated a wigwam—an Indian habitation. This was the very reason why Seward, the father of the party, was not called. God was determined to leave evidence on record sufficient to prove that he was ruling instead of man.

Again : The election campaign commences, when God makes them give Abraham a spiritual maul and wedge, and makes them call him the rail splitter. God then makes them elect him, and before the time arrives for him to start for the Chair of State the maul and wedge has cleaved off seven States from the Union. Seven rails split off, the wood is now clave for the offering, proving the South to be the wood. And in further proof of this, the first State split off has a tree on its flag. You will see that this corresponds precisely with the cutting down the Liberty Tree as above.

Again : As soon as the wood was clave, Abraham saddles his ass and goes his three days' journey to where the offering was wont to be made. In the chapter on the Jewish kingdom I shall prove to you that the Union is the ass, and the Chair of State the saddle, the spirit of which started Abraham from his home to Washington, in sight of the place where the offering was wont to be made. He however was more than three days going, but it is not more than a three days' journey. Since then preparation for the offering has been making, whilst the South stands in the spirit of Isaac natural, who had the wood on him and bore it to the place of the offering, which proves the North the ram, the beast, and Abraham its head. Here keep in mind that the South never cast a single electoral vote for Abraham, consequently they did not help to put the head there. Isaac did not help to put the ram on the altar. These things correspond precisely, proving the Great God to be the Ruler.

Again : Now let me ask you what becomes of the wood and the offering when made? Answer—Both disappeared ; but the wood must burn first. Just so it is that the South is now burning, and has been since Abraham arrived in sight of the place the offering was wont to be made. Now, if it was not for one peculiar feature in this offering the whole Union, North and South, would disappear in this great struggle, and that is this : Isaac was a type of Jesus, and Jesus bore the wood on him— bore His cross. So Jesus must be here before Abraham leaves the Chair of State, when he will take the wood upon Him and bear it to the place where the offering will be made. Just as true as Abraham the first and

Isaac were together when the type of this offering was set, just so true must Jesus be here before Abraham the second leaves the Chair of State. Then the ram will be caught by the horns in the thicket (thicket implies an undergrowth of timber, and horns implies power), when the offering will be completed, which will literally destroy the North, and set up God's kingdom on the germ of the seed in the woman. Now, you cannot help but see that these matters have all been typical in the Bible, and that God is coming to make the letters to the types.

Again: As further proof that Abraham was chosen to represent an Indian, I will cite you the fact that three out of every four of his warships are called by Indian names. And for the same reason an Indian spirit wished to speak to him at a spiritual circle held at his mansion some months since. All this proves that God makes Abraham act to fill the place of an Indian. Also, as further proof that the South is the wood, I will cite you the fact that they kept the Union army at bay for more than six months with wooden cannon placed in position—pine logs in the place of cannon. And further, a thousand wooden muskets were found in Tennessee. You may rest assured that all these things have not happened by chance. I do not name these things because I find fault; no, but to show you that you are carrying out the plans of God.

Now, whilst on this subject, I will notice the new power in the germ of the seed, and standing in the woman. Let us test it by the sowing of seed, as Paul illustrates the Resurrection. Suppose you plant a grain of corn and the germ sprouts and grows, what becomes of the life in the body of the grain? Answer—It goes into the germ and makes a new stalk, and the grain rots. Just so with the old Union. It is the grain, and the germ has sprouted; and just as certain as the life of the grain of corn goes into the germ, and the grain rot, so must every drop of life's blood in the old Union pass into the new, and the old Union rot. These are facts which no mortal man can get around. I do not want you to understand me that every man in the old Union must be killed; no, but when the seed of the woman takes the germ of the seed it must overshadow the whole land—yes, the whole world—and in that way the seed must rot, and the germ grow.

Again: Let us now be certain that this is the germ of the seed. Some men might dispute and say that the new power is not the germ of the seed. The only way you can tell the germ of the seed is by its products. You say that wheat was produced by the germ of wheat, and the same with corn, rye, and barley, and so on. This is the only way of arriving at the matter. Now, let us apply this rule to the new power. They have got a national flag with stars and stripes. They have the same constitution. They have a President and a Cabinet of seven members. They have forts and fortifications, and in fine, they have the germ of the old Union. Here again is the manifestation of God to you as the witness of His work. Had it not been the work of God they would have had everything different; they being disgusted with the old Union would not have adopted the present form of government. But having adopted it is positive proof they are not free agents, and must do the bidding of God under the veil.

I will now point you to another type set by Abraham the first. Abraham armed three hundred and eighteen servants born in his own house, and went and recaptured Lot, who had been taken prisoner by the Sodomites—Gen. 14: 14. This type, Abraham the second, was obliged to set here, standing where it ought not. I stated when he took the chair of State, that he would have to emancipate the servants and arm them, which has been fully verified. But mark, they were not born in his own house, as in this case the North elected him, and the North is his house. This will drive the South to train their servants, so when God comes in Jesus, in the Trinity set in type by Abraham, Isaac and Jacob, he will take the train of servants born in his own house, in the garden of the Lord, and recapture Lot. The South stands in the spirit of Lot, and the North in the spirit of the Sodomite kings. Then God will make the letter to the type, this train of servants will be as thorns in the sides of those who have been meddling with them, as in Judges, 2 : 33 —And their gods shall be a snare unto you. This will make an awful calamity.

I will now give this, the finishing touch. Before Abraham the first could be a full representative of the first Adam, he had to have a child born to him by a bond-woman, a black woman. This child was to represent Cain, the son of Adam, whom God made black by the curse. This son was named Ishmael, an account of which will be found in Gen. 16th ch. Now, Abraham the second must have this spirit with him in order to fully represent Abraham the first. This will be found in the Vice President, Hamlin. This will fully represent the red and black blood on the throne when Jesus comes. The seed of the woman set in type by Eve between Adam and Cain. Now, just as certain as these things stand in this connection, just so certain has Abraham got Indian blood in him, and just so certain has Hamlin got negro blood in him. By tracing Abraham's parentage back six to eight generations, you will find his mother an Indian squaw, and the same with Hamlin will prove his mother to have been a black woman.

Again : these things must be so in order to consummate the plan of God. Jesus comes the second Adam, and must occupy the place of the first Adam, now occupied by Abraham the second, and therefore must take the Book out of the right hand of Hamlin, as the type set when Jesus took the throne in Heaven—Rev. 5 : 6. Hamlin representing Ishmael, who represented Cain, who was the first son of Jesus, when first Adam. Again : the Book was a type of the Sceptre, and in place of taking the book out of the right hand of him who represents the black man, he will take the sceptre, the power which has been sealed up in the book with seven seals on the back side, which, in the next chapter, I shall prove to be the Bible, God's Book.

Again : Abraham and Ishmael, and all born in his house were circumcised in the self-same day.—Gen. 17 : 33. Ishmael was thirteen years old when he was circumcised,—25th verse. Now keep in mind that Buchanan was the thirteenth President, and that he filled the place of Pierce, who represented Judas. This leaves Buchanan's place vacant. Abraham occupies that place as the first spirit natural, that is, coming spiritual in Jesus. Hamlin will also occupy that place, and it being the thirteenth will represent the age of Ishmael when circumcised, when the letter will be made to the type set in the circumcision. This will take the veil off the upper head instead of the lower one. This is the veil which Moses put over the people, and you may rest assured it will draw a vast deal more blood than did the taking off the veil of the lower head. I have now got to the end and will leave the whole matter with you whilst I make a couple of connections and a few remarks.

Before going any further, I will notice Lot's connection with Abraham, as you will see in Genesis, 12th and 13th chapters. I pointed out this connection in the Bridegroom, but as, no doubt, many will read this who will never see that, I will also point it out here. Lot was Abraham's nephew, and therefore a cousin to Isaac, and Esau and Jacob second cousins to Ammon and Moab, two sons born to Lot by his two daughters. These two children are now represented by the kingdoms of China and Japan, as proven in the Bridegroom. Again. Isaac was a type of Jesus, the second person in the Trinity, so when Jesus stood on earth he chose the twelve Apostles who were the types of our twelve Presidents. Jesus next sent out other seventy, he sent them out two and two, without shoes, purse, or scrip.—Luke, 10th chapter. Just before the crucifixion of Jesus, he said to his disciples, " When I sent you out without purse or scrip, and shoes, lacked ye anything? And they said, Nothing. Then said he unto them, But now, he that hath a purse let him take it, and likewise his scrip, and he that hath no sword, let him sell his garment and buy one. For I say unto you, that this that is written must yet be accomplished in me. And they said, Lord, behold, here are two swords, and he said unto them, it is enough."—Luke 22: 35th to 38th verses. Soon after this Jesus was crucified, when Matthias was elected to fill the place of Judas. Keep these things in mind.

These seventy being chosen last, they will come in the Union after the twelve had been represented, and in the reign of the thirteenth, who was elected to fill the place of the twelfth. Consequently in the last year of Buchanan's reign, the Embassy from Japan arrived in this Union. They were seventy in number. They came two and two, as in that kingdom it takes two to fill an office, one to watch the other. They came without shoes, as not one of them wore shoes. They came without purse or scrip, as they came at the expense of the United States. They came bringing the very two swords which Jesus said was enough. These they left as a present at Washington, and with them the spirit of destruction, which will accomplish that that has been written, and accomplish it, too, in Jesus. Just as he stated. I suppose you will think this all chance work.

Now I will point out to you this connection. You will keep in mind that the connections above have all been made from the heads of the given points, and not the tail end. As for instance, from Adam, from Abraham, from Nebuchadnezzar, and Jesus, and the Pope. But this connection brings in the tail end of the antedeluvian world. Lot was the son of Haron, who was the third spirit in the Trinity, out of which Abraham was chosen as first spirit in the Trinity of God's kingdom, as in Genesis, 11 chapter. This placed Lot as the spirit of the ghost dead in the devil. Hence this Embassy from Japan arrives here in the last year of Buchanan's reign. Keep in mind in the above connections, that Buchanan represented the ghost dead in the devil. This is the reason why Buchanan did not connect with Nebuchadnezzar. Nebuchadnezzar had his son as live ghost, hence he connects with Abraham, who represents Esau, who was live ghost for the devil. Buchanan also connects with the Pope, but not directly; he stands in the spirit of Spain, which now has a woman on the throne, Spain being in the spirit of Abel dead in the devil. You will see the beauty of this connection in connecting the end of old things with the type set by the flood destroying the old world. We have now got Abraham and Lot here as just shown, and Abraham trying to conquer Lot. Again. Abraham and Lot were down in Egypt. This Embassy brings the spirit of Egypt into this Union. This brings Abraham to the chair of State, when the spirit of embalming is made manifest. I see by the papers that there are four establishments for embalming the dead in the army of Abraham. Now whilst you are embalming the dead here, they are burning up those embalmed in Egypt thousands of years ago. I suppose those embalmed here will share a similar fate. In this connection keep in mind that Jesus was also down in Egypt, in time of Herod's massacre of children.—Matthew, 2d chapter. Jesus will come whilst Abraham is making the letter to this type, in the spirit of Herod. These things, you will see, all prove true to the letter.

I proved to you that Abraham stands in the spirit of France, as also in the spirit of England, when our fathers rebelled. Louis Napoleon was the first man that took the throne of France after the tax-gatherer Louis Phillippe. Jesus will be the first man who will take this throne after the tax-gatherer Abraham. Again, the Stamp Act brought on the war with our fathers. Now this war brings on the Stamp Act, first last, and last first. Do you suppose that all these things have been chance work? Our fathers rebelled against the Stamp Act, but our fathers are not here now; but there are fathers here, and they do not rebel against the Stamp Act. This proves most conclusively that the spirit in England then is in the Union now. All the wisdom in the world cannot gainsay this.

Before going farther I must notice a type just given, set by Jesus himself. Matt. 12: 25.—And Jesus knew their thoughts, and said unto them, every kingdom divided against itself is brought to desolation, and every city or house divided against itself shall not stand. This type is now set upon earth. England is the kingdom; it was divided against itself in the birth of this Union, and has stood divided. This Union is the city divided against itself. As shown in the Bridegroom, the Union is the city mentioned by the Revelator as being four square. The South is the house now about being divided against itself. If it had its independence it would be a city, but as it has not it is only a house. Now, if Jesus uttered the truth, of which I have not the shadow of doubt, then these things cannot stand. Jesus says they shall not. Then you may be most certain that he is close at hand.

Now, when I reflect back over what I have written, I can give a pretty good guess what some of my readers will say. They will say "Thou old crazy fool, do you think you can palm such a doctrine off on the people as the truths of God's Book." Others will say, "Visionary old man, I wonder if he thinks God would choose such ignorance through whom he would speak." Whilst a few might say, "Well, I don't know why the old man may not be as near right as any of them. They all acknowledge the Bible as a mystery anyhow, and he stands as good a chance to be right as any of them." One thing they must say about the old man, that cannot be said about any other man living, viz: His doctrine is entirely original. All I have to say to this is, God says he will choose the foolishness of the world to confound the wisdom thereof, and the weakness to confound the strength. Reader, when you look over these connections and compare them all carefully with the Bible, you cannot help but see that we have got in this Union, standing where it ought not, the spirit of all the barbarous kingdoms ever existing on earth. Yes, we don't even stop here, but go back beyond the flood and get the spirit of all the tribes then existing, when the wickedness of man had become so great that God had to destroy them with a flood, as type set in Gen., 6th chapter. God is now coming to destroy this wickedness with the seven vials of his wrath, set in type as the seven extra heats of Nebuchadnezzar's furnace. We have got the murderers set in type by Cain the first murderer. We have also got the devil set in type in him, as given by Jesus. We have got the thieves in connection with the murderer, and devil. There is scarcely a contractor in the army but what is a thief and robber, not speaking of those outside. Almost all transactions between man and man have the spirit of thief and robber about them. Besides we have the father of lies here; the same called by Jesus a liar from the beginning, and of whom the Revelator said should be locked in the bottomless pit for a thousand years, and then loosed for a little season. This little season has arrived, standing where it ought not, and from that time the father of lies has been in full blast. Not one-tenth part of the dispatches received from him are true. To-day a dispatch came that contradicted the one of yesterday in many parts. To-morrow one will come contradicting the one of to-day; and thus it has been going on ever since the father of lies has been loose. Mark, I am not finding fault with this. I know it must be so. I know it cannot be helped. I blame no one. Every one is doing God's will. Were it not so these things set in type six thousand years ago could not now be so completely fulfilling.

Here I will close this chapter as stated above, and notice the twenty-three hundred days mentioned in Daniel 8 : 14, in connection with Millerism. You will see that I have not brought it in in my illustration at all. You will see that I have made no calculation by figures to come to the conclusion at which I have arrived. Millerism is based entirely upon figures, and they say the only difficulty in calculation is that they don't know when the twenty-three hundred days commence. Miller, the founder of the doctrine of Millerism, thought he had the time to an hour. But the poor fellow was disappointed for all that. The day came but no Jesus came. Now, twenty years have nearly gone by, and they are still harping on Millerism. Now, I would like for some of these wise men to tell the community how a doctrine proving false twenty years ago could be any evidence of Jesus coming now, or at any future period. I think such a thing is an absurdity. Any doctrine that Jesus has proven as false as this one should never be brought to light by thinking men. Most certainly none of His children would attempt it; and none but those who are ignorant of the doctrine would do it, inasmuch as it could be no evidence of His coming. Jesus may come in a month for all I know, and I know He will come before Abraham leaves the throne; but Millerism don't give me that evidence, neither can it give any body else that evidence.

I will now give these people the starting point for the twenty-three hundred days, and I will tell them how I received it. Some three months since I was in conversation with a lady friend on the subject of this doctrine, in the course of which Millerism came up, when she informed me that she had been to hear several lectures on Millerism. She said the speaker stated the only difficulty they had in setting the precise time of the coming of Jesus, was the starting point for the twenty-three hundred days; when she asked me if I knew the starting point. I told her that I had received the connections invariably without the twenty-three hundred days. And in my connections the abominations of desolation, which was to cleanse the sanctuary, must be set up in the year 1866, by France conquering England. And I thought the twenty-three hundred days were only placed there to puzzle the wisdom of the world. I further stated that with my present knowledge on the prophecy of Daniel I could soon find out the starting point.

Time passed on and I thought no more of the matter. Some four or five weeks after, I was sitting smoking my pipe, and not thinking of these matters at all, when all of a sudden, the division of the seventy weeks, in the 9th ch., was put on my tongue as the starting point for the twenty-three hundred days, something in this manner : The division of the seventy weeks is the beginning of the days. The idea was immediately given me **that** the division of the seventy weeks was the beginning of the twenty-three hundred days. I knew how the weeks were divided, as I had in Miller's time, tried to make some calculation myself, but all to no purpose. The seventy weeks are divided as follows : first, seven weeks, then three score and two weeks, and then one week—Daniel, 9 : 25. I then cast up in my mind the three score and two weeks, and found it to be four hundred and thirty-four years. Then I added that and 1866 together, in my mind, as follows : Eighteen and four make twenty-two, and thirty-four and sixty-six make one hundred; added to the twenty-two, made twenty-three. And thus I found it the starting point for the twenty-three hundred days, closing with the year 1866, the very year God had given me before, giving me double evidence of the truth of my doctrine, and that they were placed there to puzzle the wisdom of the world.

After I had finished smoking I went to my room and took my Bible, and found in it everything as given me. I then, in order to reconcile the matter with the date of the vision in which the twenty-three hundred days are mentioned, added the seven weeks, or forty-nine years, to the four hundred and thirty-four, and then added the seventy years, in 9th ch. 2d verse, which gave me just 553 years before Christ, the very year in which the vision was had in which Daniel overheard the saints speaking of the time, and the answer twenty-three hundred days. Then the idea was given me thus : If this be correct, then the walls of Jerusalem must have been rebuilt, and the Israelites back again in Jerusalem, just four hundred and thirty-four years before Christ. I then turned to the last dates in the book of Neh., and found it precisely four hundred and thirty-four years, and thus every difficulty in the prophecy of Daniel harmonized. Now my friends, the Millerites can get the true starting point for the twenty-three hundred days, direct from their God. And they can see that Daniel the second, was right in placing their end in the year 66, without a knowledge of the twenty-three hundred days. Daniel's God is never wrong.

Again : this makes the year 1863 the year when the daily sacrifice and the sanctuary shall be given to desolation, and trodden under foot, which will cleanse the Sanctuary, as in Daniel, 8 : 13, 14. The daily sacrifice referred to here was that set in type by the sacrificing of beasts in the Jewish kingdom, before the throne of God. When Pagan Rome destroyed the Jewish kingdom, they received the spirit of this sacrifice, which was probably modified some. This spirit was transferred to Papal Rome. and has been continued to the present day. Henry the eighth, the son of the Pope spiritual, changes the form of worship a little, which he called the high church of England. This was the stepping stone to Protestantism. The same, or similar sacrifices have been continued in the high church of England unto this day. A number of branches of these worships are in the Union, in which those sacrifices are offered. The sacrificing of beasts before the throne of God, was typical of the destruction of human life, in the spirit of the beast, when God comes to take His throne on earth. This has now commenced with Abraham standing where it ought not, and when the calamity has passed over, the Sanctuary will be closed. Five, six or seven hundred million of human beings swept from earth by wars, plagues, famines and pestilence, in the spirit of the beast, will cleanse the world, which is the Sanctuary referred to, set in type by the most holy place in the Tabernacle. This is tho truo state of affairs. Then prepare to meet your God, for bchold, the Bridegroom cometh. My doctrine is not mine, but His that sent me.

I will now pay a brief notice to the teachings of those people, showing there is no truth in them. This I might however dispense with, inasmuch as if God is now with Daniel, it proves Millerism, as well as all other isms, false; nevertheless I shall proceed to the task. These people teach that God is coming to take his saints away in the clouds, and burn up the world and wicked, and at the end of a thousand years He is coming back to earth, when He will find the earth purified and made fit for Him 'and His people. Then He will resurrect the whole world of mankind, and judge them, to know whether they have merited their punishment, and all who have He will send back to hell, there to suffer through endless ages, and those who have not He will send as parched cracklings to Heaven to enjoy Him. Now, I ask, what would men think of a Judge on earth who would condemn his prisoners and send them to punishment, before knowing whether guilty or not. They would certainly displace him very quick. To this no doubt they will say, God knows all things beforehand. If so, why call them to trial at all.

Again: They say that God is a God of love, mercy and justice. Just think of such a God forcing billions of millions of human beings into existence, then for a few years of sin, which they have been forced into, force them out of existence, and force them into an endless hell, there to roast in endless flames. Why, sir, such a God as that could not be equaled by the boiling down and double distilling and concentrating into one being all the devils ever having existed on earth. Such a devil would be an object of love and adoration, beside such a God. What would you think of a father who would torment a child forty years for the sin of a single year? Why, sirs, you would say that he was a perfect demon, yet upon the same principle you say such a God is a God of love and mercy. Away with such trash. It was right in its day, as the devil has been God's right hand man, and as God has been bringing good out of evil, he gave the devil this doctrine to frighten those who would be the wickedest without, and thereby bring good out of evil. By this you can tell what all the people would have been who believe this doctrine. God is now coming to take the devil's place, when all the doctrines of the devil must be swept from earth, together with himself, and God with the doctrine given Daniel, stand in his place. Enough on this head.

The strongest passage they have in the Bible to prove that God is coming to take His saints away, will be found in 1st Thes. 4: 16, 17. "For the Lord himself shall descend from Heaven with a shout, with the voice of an archangel, and with the trump of God, and the dead in Christ shall rise first. Then we which are alive and remain, shall be caught up together with them in the clouds, to meet the Lord in the air, and so shall we ever be with the Lord." You will see here that there is nothing said about the Lord coming in the clouds. Daniel saw one like the son of man come in the clouds. Jesus tells us himself that He will come in the clouds of Heaven.

The Revelator also says he cometh with clouds, 1: 7. Now as this coming does not take place in the clouds, it is not the coming referred to by the Revelator, Jesus or Daniel. But is the same referred to by the Revelator in 16: 15, which I shall in the next chapter prove will take place when Jesus comes from this Union, which will be his heaven then, to the old world, to fight the battle of Armageddon. Being received in the cloud was set in type by Moses. He ascended a mountain to enter the cloud. This mountain was the type of God's kingdom. So when God comes in the cloud, and has set up his kingdom, it will represent the mountain. The people who compose his kingdom will have been elevated from the power of the devil to God, as was Moses elevated when on the mountain. The cloud will be manifested frequently during the setting up of the kingdom, as it was in the wilderness, and a great manifestation made when the throne is moved to England, as was the case when Solomon dedicated the temple of old Jerusalem. The resurrection implied in the passage is simply the quickening to newness of life those who shall be accounted worthy of the kingdom, which will shake off the elements of the devil. They frequently quote another passage of Scripture to show the destruction of the world. 2. Peter, 3: 10, 12. "But the day of the Lord will come as a thief in the night, in the which the heavens shall pass away with a great noise, and the elements shall melt with fervent heat, the earth also and the works that are therein shall be burned up. Looking forward and hasting unto the coming of the day of God, wherein the heavens being on fire shall be dissolved, and the elements shall melt with fervent heat." I would simply ask now, if the heavens mentioned here are the heavens above, and the elements the atmosphere we breathe, where, in the name of heaven, will the cloud take the saints to? I proved in the Bridegroom that the Union was the heaven, or kingdom of heaven, and the flag the new heaven seen by the Revelator. And now the germ has come out of the seed producing another flag with stars. This makes heavens, the plural. These heavens are now passing away with a great noise. The noise of cannon, mortars, muskets, drums, and armies tramping, all combined, make the great noise referred to, and when the Lord sends forth the noise of his artillery, it finishes it up. The elements referred to here are those of the devil, they must pass away with the devil, by the seven extra heats of Nebuchadnezzar sealed up in the seven vials of God's wrath, the fire of which has already been kindled in the South, from where it must spread all over the world. The earth referred to here is man made of earth, out of which all things on earth have come, that is, all things that have been made by the hand of man, which are to be burned up with this fire, and new things take their place.

Again. In Isaiah, 34: 4, 5, we have the following: "And all the hosts of heaven shall be dissolved, and the heavens shall be rolled together as a scroll, and all their hosts shall fall down, as the leaf falleth off from the vine, and as the falling fig from the fig tree. For my sword shall be bathed in heaven; behold it shall come down upon Idumea and of the people of my curse to judgment. This is another passage quoted by this people as proving their doctrine. The heavens are to be rolled together as a scroll. Rolling up anything makes it occupy a small space. That is just what is being done now with these heavens, and when all the hosts of them fall down as the leaf from the vine, when two thirds of the people are swept from the earth, then these heavens can occupy a much smaller place. The Lord here says his sword shall be bathed in heaven. I wonder if this is the heaven these people are going to in the cloud. If so, it cannot be a much holier place than here. They do not believe this Union is the heaven in which this passage is now being fulfilled, and before the strife ends, God will be here and bathe his sword in it, and therefore they must believe that it is the heaven they are going to, or the one God will set up when he brings them back to earth. In either case it would not be a better one than the one we are now living in. Thus it is with all these Scriptures when properly explained.

Once more. These people tell you that if you do not keep the seventh day as the Sabbath, you have the mark of the beast. This is the most singular thing yet come to light. How keeping the first day of the week for the Sabbath, can give any one the mark of the beast, I am at a loss to know. One thing I do know, the seventh day was the Lord's day, hence He gave it to his chosen people for a Sabbath, and for them it is their only true Sabbath. But for my life, I cannot find any place where He tells me that He gave that day to any Gentile for a Sabbath. I also find that God begat Jesus, and furthermore, that He had set himself in type in the midst of the six branches of the golden candlestick, in the main candlestick as seventh. Hence, His Son, Jesus, is the eighth in the midst of the seven candlesticks, and therefore his Sabbath would be what would be to the Jews the eighth day, or the first day of the week. I also find that Jesus was crucified on Friday, and the spirit of God absent on Saturday, the Jewish Sabbath, and again made its appearance on the first day of the Jewish week, which becomes the Gentile Sabbath, the Sabbath of Jesus, the resurrection day of Jesus, and of all other days, the one most befitting his followers to keep as the Sabbath.

Again. Jesus chose twelve Jews, and afterward conferred himself upon Saul of Tarsus, when he chose twelve Gentiles. This was the spiritual type of the union of the Jew and Gentile nations. Now, when Jesus comes to make the letter to this type, God in his seven spirits, which was the type of the seventh as the Jewish Sabbath, will be in him, and when he confers himself upon the Gentile world, as the type set in Saul, then all the world must come into His Sabbath. As the Father comes in the Son, so the Jews must come into the Son's Sabbath. Then I wonder where those Gentiles will be who have fled to the Jews to get rid of the "mark of the beast." The very fact that they flee to the Jews, implies that they have the "mark of the beast," and wish to erase it by fleeing there. There is no possible evidence to be found proving that the Jews will retain their present Sabbath when the Messiah comes. No, they themselves look for a change when that day comes. They believe in the Triune God, the God of Abraham, Isaac and Jacob. This God being a Triune God, He must come in the second person, which brings the first, as also the third spirit, into the second. This will bring all things into the second—into Jesus, or Messiah. Now, just as true as the Jews are right in their Sabbath, just so true is a Gentile in the spirit or "mark of the beast," when he takes the Jewish Sabbath to escape it. Let this suffice on this point.

I will now draw my remarks to a close, as the reader can see that there can be no evidence brought to prove such doctrine. God having spoken the Bible through man, and now explaining them through man, must prove all other interpretations false. These people make all their calculations from the prophecy of Daniel. I wish now they would tell you how God will set up the kingdom of which Daniel prophecied, by taking his saints to another world. Daniel says he shall set up his kingdom in the days of these kings. They say he will take his people away and destroy these kings. I would like to know how this would be setting up the kingdom in the days of these kings. For Daniel, if he means what he says, means that these kings shall live whilst the kingdom in question is being set up. Furthermore, how can the kingdom set up break in pieces and consume all these kingdoms unless it is set up where those kingdoms are, viz—on earth. For most certainly Daniel means by breaking in pieces and consuming all these kingdoms, the destruction of them as kingdoms, and the uniting into God's kingdom such portions of them as he may choose. This is the only way the kingdom and dominion, and the greatness of the kingdom under the whole heaven, can be given to the people of the saints of the Most High, as in Dan. 7 : 27. I ask again how can this be done if the world, together with these kingdoms, is destroyed? Again, how can the stone become a great mountain filling the whole earth, as in Dan. 2 : 25, if the earth is destroyed? or how will the taking of the saints to heaven fill the whole earth? Such ideas are perfectly ridiculous when compared with the prophecy of Daniel.

A few words more and I leave these people to travel in the dark path with the veil over their eyes. Some two years ago, when the paper called the "World's Crisis" was about going into operation, and having a slight acquaintance with the editor, I concluded it would be a good chance to get some short articles published. So meeting the editor in the street one day, I asked him if he would publish a short article occasionally, stating that I had tried many editors, but all refused as I had no money to pay for publishing. He said if I would prop up my arguments with Scriptural proofs he would publish some for me. I then wrote out a very brief article on the subject of the New Jerusalem, as in the first chapter of the Bridegroom, and left it with him for some ten days, when I again received it with a refusal to publish it. I asked him to give me his reasons for refusing to publish it. He then said your doctrine is so entirely new that I must refuse to publish it. "It is a doctrine," said he, "that no other man has ever attempted to prove from the Scriptures, and I can't consistently publish any thing but what has been advanced by Ministers of the Gospel in present and former ages." I then said unto him the Bible teaches that old things must pass away and new things must take their places, and that an old doctrine could not usher in a new era in the history of the world; that it would require a new doctrine to usher in a new era in the history of the world, and that I thought that he had better publish it. But no; he said he would publish nothing but old things; and thus I left him. I have since seen several of his papers, and find he holds his own very well, his paper being continually filled with old matter. Not a word of new in it. Well, I don't blame him. The Lord don't give him anything new, and the devil has none to give, and therefore he must be satisfied with what he has. Peace be with him!

I thought of closing here, but the Lord says I must show them that their hell is a false one, and the only hell he has is the grave. The grave is the natural hell, and dragon's reign is the spiritual hell. There is a natural hell, and a spiritual hell. A natural devil, and a spiritual devil. And a natural heaven, and a spiritual heaven. And a natural God, and a spiritual god. These things are all true, as I shall now prove.

In Revelation, 1 : 18, we have the following words, from him that sat in the midst of the seven golden candlesticks : "I am He that liveth and was dead, and behold, I am alive forevermore, Amen, and have the keys of death and of hell." You see that this personage was Jesus. He has the keys of death and of hell. A man having keys, implies that he has something locked up with them. So with Jesus; he has the keys of hell and death. Now, when He comes He will unlock death and hell. How will He unlock them? Simply by slaying men. We know of death in no sense, only by the destruction of life ; this constitutes death. So, if after Jesus comes, a hundred die to one now, then death will be unlocked, and will roam about doing its work. Suppose you had a hundred murderers locked up in prison, and you was to unlock the prison, the murderers would roam at large, and murderers would be plenty, a hundred to where would not be one if kept locked up; just so with death. This unlocking of death unlocks hell, makes subjects for the grave. For every additional hundred of deaths, you must have the same number of graves. This places death and hell together, death in hell, hence Jesus has the keys of both.

Again: Rev. 6: 8. "I looked and beheld a pale horse, and his name was Death, and hell followed with him." This, you will see, took place when the fourth seal of the book was opened in Heaven. Now, keep in mind that this same personage who had the keys of hell and death, took the throne in Heaven, and opened the seals of the book, and when the fourth seal was opened, Death was the name of him on the pale horse, and hell followed with him. Here you see that the seven seals of the book were the locks, and he unlocked them with the keys. This sets the type of death and hell loose in Heaven. So when Jesus comes and takes the throne on earth, but still in the Heaven in which the type was set, as the Revelator saw it descend out of Heaven from God, he will make the letter to the type, when death being loose, will follow with him on the pale horse, when hell will follow with the army. Most certainly an endless hell in a future world can't follow anybody. Reader, you certainly can't help but see this.

Once more—Isaiah, 14: 9. "Hell from beneath is moved for thee to meet thee at thy coming; it stirreth up the dead for thee, even all the chief ones of the earth, it hath raised up from their thrones all the kings of the nations." This passage, you will see, stands in connection with the cutting down of Lucifer, son of the morning, and casting the abominable branch out without a burial. This Lucifer is the people, and the branch the Church. This takes place at the battle of Armageddon, when millions will be slain with the seven vials of wrath, through the world, as in Jer. 25: 33. "And the slain of the Lord shall be in that day, from one end of the earth, even unto the other end of the earth, they shall not be lamented, neither gathered, nor buried. They shall be dung upon the earth." This is why the prophet said, "Hell has come up to meet you. You don't dig graves to bury them; they rot upon the earth. Hell has come up on top of the earth." Thus, you can't help but see that the grave is the Scripture hell, and that Jesus has the keys to both. If our friends' doctrine of God burning up the earth with all the kingdoms on it, be true, then these people mentioned here as cast out without a burial, can't become dung upon the earth; hence the prophet will have lied. I could cite you to many more Scriptures on this subject, but let this suffice for the present.

The dragon's kingdom is spiritual hell. The dragon is that spirit which makes man a devil natural. And when men confer that spirit upon one man by votes, or any other process, and make him rule over them, then he stands as spiritual devil, and his reign is spiritual hell—such as we are now in—and such as the whole world will be in before this strife closes. I stated above that the Democratic party stood as God natural. When they placed a man in power to rule over them, then he ruled in the spirit of the natural God, and the people he would govern would constitute heaven natural. That spirit ruling during the thirteen Presidents, makes it heaven. This heaven has now become spiritual hell. So when spiritual God comes and destroys spiritual hell, by destroying that spirit that makes it such, then it will be spiritual heaven, and God in it, and natural hell filled to overflowing. This is the sum of the matter in a few words.

I will now close by stating that the chapter on the Revelation, will doubly prove all I have here stated. Besides, it will show the connection of the throne of England with a number of our Presidents, at least with every one from Polk to Abraham, showing that the fulfillment of the Revelation will be the setting up of God's kingdom. And in that chapter, the connections with Daniel's prophecy will be again pointed out.

Adieu, for the present.

DANIEL LEIBEE.

www.ingramcontent.com/pod-product-compliance
Lightning Source LLC
Chambersburg PA
CBHW021519090426
42739CB00007B/684